TEACHING WRITING: A Systematic Approach

DATE			

TEACHING WRITING

Colin Peacock

CROOM HELM

London • Sydney • Dover, New Hampshire

© 1986 Colin Peacock
Croom Helm Ltd, Provident House, Burrell Row,
Beckenham, Kent BR3 1AT

Croom Helm Australia Pty Ltd, Suite 4, 6th Floor,
64-76 Kippax Street, Surry Hills, NSW 2010, Australia

British Library Cataloguing in Publication Data

Peacock, Colin
    Teaching writing: a systematic
    approach.
    1. English language — Rhetoric —
    Study and teaching (Secondary)
    I. Title
    808'.042'071   LB1631

    ISBN 0-7099-4028-9

Croom Helm, 51 Washington Street, Dover,
New Hampshire 03820, USA

Library of Congress Cataloging in Publication Data
applied for

Printed and bound in Great Britain
by Billing & Sons Limited, Worcester.

CONTENTS

List of Figures
Preface and Acknowledgements

1. TEACHING WRITING: A CONTEXT FOR
CHANGE................................. 1

2. WRITING AND THE COMMUNICATION OF
MEANING................................ 11

Speech and Writing..................... 12
Categories of Writing................. 16
The Teaching of Writing: A Cognitive
Approach............................... 18

3. THE WRITING PROCESS: AN ANALYSIS........ 24

Composing.............................. 26
Transcribing........................... 30
Reviewing.............................. 34

4. THE FORMATIVE ASSESSMENT OF WRITING..... 37

Kevin's Difficulties: 'Let's Play
Poison'................................ 38
The Nature of Formative Assessment...... 42
Identifying Strengths and Weaknesses.... 50
Managing Formative Assessment in the
Classroom.............................. 54

5. PRE-WRITING ACTIVITIES.................. 57

The Level of Difficulty................ 59
Defining the Nature and Purpose of the
Task................................... 63

	Criteria for Success.....................	66
	Using a Model of Success.................	70
	Planning.................................	71
	The Role of Discussion...................	73
6.	HELPING CHILDREN TO IMPROVE AS WRITERS..	77
	Drafting and Redrafting..................	78
	Showing..................................	84
	Practice.................................	92
	Discriminating...........................	95
	Solving Problems.........................	100
7.	SUCCESS IN WRITING: THEORY AND PRACTICE	105
	The Concept of Success...................	106
	Classroom Methodology....................	109
	Case Study: 'First Day at Secondary School'.................................	114
	Pre-Writing......................	117
	Drafting and Redrafting.........	121
8.	CONCLUSION: IMPLICATIONS FOR PROFESSIONAL PRACTICE................................	129
Appendices....................................		135
References....................................		138
Index...		142

FIGURES

4.1   Kevin's Script: 'Let's Play Poison'....   39
4.2   Profile for Assessment.................   49

5.1   Checklist for Writing Task: 'Boy
      Meets Girl'............................   67
5.2   Planning Map: 'Boy Meets Girl'........   74

6.1   Adele's Second Draft..................   81
6.2   'Rescue Groups Ease the Crisis' :
      Pupil's Plan and First Draft...........   99

7.1   Constituent Elements of Classroom
      Rationale..............................   115
7.2   Sequence of Classroom Activities
      Leading to Summative Evaluation.......   116
7.3   Worksheet: the Move from Primary to
      Secondary School......................   119
7.4   Autobiographical Assignment: Checklist
      of Criteria for Success...............   120
7.5   Pupil's Planning Map.................   122
7.6   Summative Assessment Profile..........   124

PREFACE AND ACKNOWLEDGEMENTS

The chapters that follow are about developing
children's skills as writers in the late primary,
middle and secondary school, not about the initial
teaching of the 'basic skills' of letter formation
and sentence construction. The book is about theory
as well as about professional practice and it is
addressed both to the classroom teacher of writing
and to those likely to influence their beliefs and
practices.
     The book has been written as a result of wide
professional experience and growing personal knowledge and understanding, and it expresses, I
believe, a distinctive point of view about the teaching of writing in schools. I have endeavoured to
set my arguments in the context of the realities and
pressures of classroom life, and I have drawn on my
own experience as a classroom teacher, on the
evidence supplied by teachers (from both primary
and secondary schools) with whom I have worked on
in-service courses, on classroom observation and
interviews with experienced teachers, and on classroom action-research. I am also fortunate to have
worked closely on the development of interdisciplin-
ary courses in teacher education with colleagues in
the Department of Education, University of Stirling.
This collaboration has undoubtedly influenced the
rationale for the teaching of writing that is
expounded, discussed and illustrated.
     In writing the book, therefore, I would like
to acknowledge a particular debt to the following
individuals:
- Professor Arnold Morrison and Angela Roger with
  whom I worked closely on the project funded by
  the Scottish Education Department *Language Skills
  in English: Writing at Foundation Level*

- Teachers from primary and secondary schools in Central Scotland with whom I have collaborated and whose classroom work is described and discussed, especially Lilian Challinor, John Hart, John McKeown, and Mary Reid

- Members of the secretarial staff of the Department of Education, University of Stirling, Meg Carroll and Dorothy Kelly, and especially Irene Lindsay who has typed the final camera-ready copy

- Lyn North, graphics artist at the University of Stirling, for her help with the art work

That said, the arguments developed in the book and the conclusions reached are, of course, my own and I take full responsibility for them.

Chapter One

TEACHING WRITING : A CONTEXT FOR CHANGE

For many years now I have thought of myself as a
teacher of writing. Although my classroom experience
does not include the earliest stages when the basic
skills of letter formation and the creation and
transcription of simple sentences are first taught
and learned in the primary school, over the years I
have attempted to help a variety of children, young
people and adults to consolidate and develop the
skills in writing they have already acquired. Some
of the pupils I have taught have been competent or
talented writers; many though have been lacking in
self-confidence when they approached a writing task
and have been self-denigrating about their achievements; a small number have struggled to produce even
a single legible sentence.
    No one ever fully 'masters' the skills involved
in writing; there is no identifiable agreed threshold
which a beginner writer has to reach in order to be
recognised as a skilled practitioner. Improvement
and development are realistic goals for even the most
able and talented writers. As with reading, we should
all of us be learning to write all our lives. But in
the course of my experience as a classroom teacher I
became increasingly aware of how difficult it appeared
to be to help children to improve significantly as
writers. And when faced with their problems I offered
a variety of different explanations and solutions to
myself, to parents, and to colleagues in order to
clarify or to help overcome our shared difficulties.
    Every day in school we had to deal with children
of differing abilities who had reached varied levels
of attainment, and it was tempting to explain failure
or apparent lack of progress in a child's writing
development in terms of what pupils appeared to lack.
They did not possess sufficient intelligence or
general ability; they lacked motivation in school and

a supportive home background; there was no encouragement to read and write at home and children heard
little in the way of elaborated conversation from
their parents or peers. None of these explanations
at the time seemed adequate, no matter how persuasive
or partially true they are. Instead I came to
examine more critically my own lack of professional
understanding concerning the demands placed on a
beginning writer when he or she struggled to make
the marks on the page and communicate a message in
writing. And I am now more critical too of the ways
in which I organised learning in the classroom, how
I planned and implemented work, the kinds of help I
provided for individual children and how progress
was assessed and evaluated.

Many teachers of writing, probably, begin their
careers, as I did, with a body of largely untested
beliefs and limited professional skills and have in
the main to learn as best they can from the successes
they achieve in the classroom and the mistakes they
make. For my own part, I tried to establish a classroom climate that was relaxed and informal so that
pupils could talk to each other and to me with
reasonable freedom and could enjoy their work. I
believed (as an article of faith) that children
become literate and develop their skills in reading
and writing by actually engaging in these activities
as total experiences, not by mastering isolated skills
in handwriting, sentence and paragraph construction,
spelling and punctuation, through a programme of
decontextualised exercises. Although there were
cupboards full of textbooks of varying ages which
gave explanations about and practice in writing
skills, I would not (I vowed) be reduced to using
them. Other classes might be quite content to work
their way through them, filling in blanks, copying
out sentences and answering questions, but my pupils
would learn to write by writing. It was essential,
I argued, to encourage pupils to write at length, to
make the effort to express what they wanted to say
in their own words and in their own way.

The most important classroom role I had to play
was, I believed, that of enthusiast and motivator.
I had to create situations in the classroom with a
variety of stimuli which led via discussion to the
pupils writing, and I needed to choose topics that
were close to the lives, experiences and interests of
the children. As regards the errors that were being
made by members of the class when they wrote and the
problems that were being experienced, I needed to
intervene during and after the process of writing to

offer help to individual pupils, to respond to the
errors that were being made and to suggest ways of
overcoming them.
    Fortunately some children experienced few
difficulties, if any at all, in communicating their
meaning through the medium of the written word. From
an early age in their school careers they were on the
way to becoming successful writers. For example,
supported by classroom discussion and having been
given a clear sense of purpose and audience for her
task, Lesley (aged 12) produced the following short
piece of writing. It is not presented as an outstanding example of children's imaginative writing,
simply a successful piece of classroom work with an
assured sense of story and atmosphere.

MOMENT OF FEAR

*I was all alone that night, that is, the only
person in the house. You know, when you are
alone at night everything seems to creak or make
some sort of frightening noise. But when someone is with you, you think nothing of it.*

    *Since it was a cold, windy night, I had my
windows clamped shut. The wind was howling round
the house, and leaves were constantly scraping
against the window. I was snuggled down in bed
with two hot water bottles, one on either side of
me, when I heard a loud creak. Stiffening, I
snuggled down even further into the warm blankets.
Then I firmly told myself, 'Don't be so ridicul-
ous. Of course there is an explanation to that
n..noise. It's probably just... just...' But I
could not think any more, for just then came yet
another creak. I told myself again 'Be sensible,
be SENSIBLE. It's nothing. Probably just a
window left open somewhere and the door being
blown.' Then it dawned on me. 'Oh, NO. Not a
window left open, please, please don't let it be
a window left open.'*

    *Then there was a slow pad, padding up the
stairs. I gasped with fright, very quietly
stepped out of bed, tip-toed to my bookcase, and
chose four heavy books. Then I tip-toed to my
dressing table and grabbed a hair-brush. Now I
was armed, but what could I do? Ah, the wardrobe
was the answer, I crept over and opened the door.
Just as I was climbing in, my bedroom door opened.
I always left it open a crack anyway. I sprang
back into bed, dropping the books as I went.
Then something jumped on top of me. Of course,
I had been thoroughly stupid. It was my pet*

3

> *puppy who had been frightened by the wind and
> had come up to be comforted.*

If Lesley and pupils like her are offered a subject
that is close to their experience and interests (after
all, everyone has been afraid at some time in their
lives), are given some kind of stimulus and support
before they begin to write, they usually experience
no serious difficulties. Lesley, for example, could
formulate and express the meanings she wished to
communicate. She had read widely for pleasure from
an early age and her writing shows an assured sense
of story-telling and a confidence in using an informal register of narrative prose. She was also a
fluent talker and played a lively part in class
discussion. In putting pen to paper she knew what
was expected of her, told her story well and
experienced no problems with the mechanics of writing
or the conventions of spelling and punctuation.
     Pupils like Lesley do seem to 'learn to write
by writing'. And it was easy to accept that what was
appropriate to her was in principle appropriate to
all pupils. As long as the teacher takes care in
selecting a topic, presents some kind of stimulus
and provides support with classroom discussion and
explanation, the interest that is engendered will
motivate children to write. Pupils will be carried
forward by their own involvement in the task with a
desire to communicate a personal message to the
reader especially if some kind of final publication
or shared reading is involved. Any problems they
encounter can be solved incidentally with help from
the teacher or their peers in the course of their
gradual and increasing mastery of the writing system.
Teachers need only to provide encouragement, give
their pupils a sense of purpose and audience for
their writing and help to sort out individual difficulties as they occur. The writer's message is all
important; other features of the writing system will
fall into place in the course of time with practice
and growing experience.
     These were some of the arguments I put forward
and the beliefs I initially held about the teaching
of writing. In many ways they worked well for some
pupils and I did not feel any sense of challenge or
threat in dealing with the mass of less successful
children, until, that is, I took over responsibility
for 2G. 2G is one class in my teaching experience
I think I shall never forget. I was in my first
year at a new school after five years' teaching
experience elsewhere and the class in question was

4

the lowest stream of seven groups. It contained a dozen or so children (also aged about twelve years) all of whom had been categorised as remedial; most of them were still experiencing serious problems with reading and writing. There was at that time neither a remedial department in the school nor a specialist remedial teacher. I was to be partly responsible for their work in English.

The children in 2G were clearly not without ability. Ruth took great delight in drawing and colouring illustrations for her written work that were skilful and imaginative; James and Neil were enthusiasts and experts on the subject of lorries and would have happily spent all their time in the classroom drawing immaculate blueprint plans of different kinds of artics; Leonard played in the school rugby team. But most of them seemed at best semi-literate. Their reading and writing problems were quite beyond my professional competence and experience. I approached the situation and their difficulties in the only way I could, using the beliefs, classroom skills and knowledge I already possessed, picking up any advice I could from written or oral sources, and improvising (with varying degrees of success).

My approach was not a total failure. The class and I got on reasonably well together and they seemed to enjoy their year's work in English. I adopted a topic or thematic approach to their writing and they worked quite hard for short bursts of time at well-tried topics like 'The Island Story' and 'My World' (a series of pieces about their family, neighbourhood and friends), and the following composite effort followed a trip by coach to the Tower of London.

> *2G VISIT THE TOWER OF LONDON*
> *On February 27th 2G went to London. The coach arrived at school at nine-thirty. It was a nice journey, the weather was hot but there was a breeze. We went from school to the M1. We left the M1., where cars and lorries had passed us and arrived in London at twelve o'clock.*
> Juisephine, Geraldine
>
> *We parked near the Tower of London and bought our tickets to go inside. Outside the Tower was a guard at his sentry-box. We went inside the Tower and a Beefeater showed us the Bloody Tower. We went inside the Bloody Tower and saw the portcullis mechanism. Then we were told we could go anywhere.*
> Ruth

5

So Ruth and I went to see the White Tower and
the guns and swords.   There was men's armour,
armour for horses and even a suit of armour for
an elephant.   The place where all these are
kept is called the Armoury.

Dianna

I remember best of all the different kinds of
guns.   There was a Gatling gun.   It holds fifty
bullets.   There was a mortar, a double twelve
bore, a single twelve bore and a cannon.

Neil

I got lost and Robin and Michael with me.   They
went into one place and I went up where the
Crown Jewels were to see if Miss Barwick was
there.   She was not, so I ran down the stairs
and looked for Robin and Michael, but I could
not find them anywhere.   Then I saw Michael's
bobble hat.   I ran up the steps and found them
all.

Noel

I was lost in the Bloody Tower.   Inside it was
dark and creepy.   In a dungeon there was a
stretching machine on which they put the prison-
ers.   There were also some narrow spiral stairs.

Robin

These stairs led up to the Crown Jewels.   They
were in a big room.   There were crowns,
bracelets, cups, swords, and many other things,
all protected by thick glass.

Michael

We went and ate our dinner down by the river.
Stephen and Donald fell off one of the cannons
and Mr Peacock said, 'Are you alright?'   They
said 'Yes'.   So we went and sat down and had
lunch.   Mr Peacock took some funny films of us.
He snapped Ruth eating a sandwich.   We saw
London Bridge open and a ship go through.

Dianna

We went back to the coach and left London at
two-thirty.   We saw Trafalgar Square, but did
not get out of the coach because it started to
rain.

Tony

> *On the way back from London we went on the M.1.*
> *We stopped at the M.1. cafe to get some refresh-*
> *ments.   I had a choc-ice, a cup of pop and some*
> *sweets.   We ran around and then went back to the*
> *coach.   When we reached school, all of us wanted*
> *to go back to London Tower.*
>
> Malcolm

This account of the trip was edited, with spelling
and punctuation corrected and emendations made to
grammar and syntax so that the piece could be pub-
lished in the school magazine. The reality of what
the pupils actually wrote in their individual reports
was quite different despite the considerable time and
trouble that were taken over the task.

It seemed convincing in other contexts to argue
that I needed to provide help and support to individual pupils during and after the process of writing,
to respond to the errors that were being made and to
suggest ways of overcoming them. But in the case of
the writing produced by 2G I felt inadequate. I
lacked an appropriate vocabulary to describe the
pupils' problems to my own satisfaction, let alone
to theirs, and I had little idea about which strategies would help them to overcome their difficulties.
I struggled along, therefore, as best I could. At
the end of the school year I could not say with any
confidence what each pupil had learned; I could not
claim any achievement that was the result of my
presence in the classroom or the programme of work
the class had followed. Although I seemed to be
successful to some extent in eventually winning
positive attitudes from the class towards their work
('We'nt got writin' 'ave we?' was a common chorus
initially), this was probably because they were
usually able to continue to do something that they
already did quite well, rather than because they were
learning to do something that they had previously
been unable to do. They loved to listen to stories
read to them rather than read for themselves, they
enjoyed colouring elaborate title pages and illustrations for stories, rather than write the stories
themselves, and they would have been happy with
improvised drama every lesson of the week.

There is no doubt that the approach I adopted
with 2G (and other more able classes) in the teaching
of writing made considerable demands on the teacher
in terms of preparation and the expenditure of nervous
energy in the classroom. Often the teacher seems to
work a good deal harder than the pupils. The approach
may help to make the classroom a happy and stimulating

place, but I now recognise that it does not necessarily help children to learn more effectively or
overcome their difficulties. I myself as a classroom
teacher lacked appropriate knowledge about the nature
of the writing process and I lacked also appropriate
professional skills which could be used to help
children to achieve more as writers and to make
progress in their writing development.

It is clear from my more recent work with
practising teachers that many of them share the values
and beliefs I have outlined, and that they adopt similar approaches to the teaching of writing in the
classroom. There is a wealth of common-sense knowledge among teachers that testifies to the failure of
traditional classroom approaches - decontextualised
exercises, spelling corrections, textbook explanations
of punctuation or sentence structure. Pupils seem to
be fairly willing and able to produce correct answers
to single, isolated problems, especially when they
are given the support of teacher, textbook or worksheet, but as most teachers of writing wearily tell
their critics who argue for a return to traditional
classroom methods, the apparently insuperable problem
is to persuade each child to apply what is learned .
in isolation (points of spelling, punctuation, style
or whatever) to the act of independent, continuous
extended writing.

It is not surprising, therefore, that in the
course of the past twenty years or so teachers have
lost faith in a structured approach to writing with
its emphasis on the mastery of skills, because the
failure of this approach seemed so apparent. Instead
they have turned to a more holistic approach which
stresses the importance of the communication of meaning through the written word, in a clear-cut context,
with a sense of purpose and a target audience. If
pupils experience difficulties within this holistic
context, then their teachers can offer on-the-spot
help as they arise or after reading and responding
to what has been written.

Traditional exercises in writing skills failed
to enable children to master the writing system so
that they could communicate their meaning in a piece
of independent, extended writing. But the alternative
holistic approach to the teaching of writing, I
believe, also has serious weaknesses. It does not
necessarily work well for the majority of pupils
still struggling to express themselves in writing
and to master the writing process's constituent
skills. The 'systematic' approach that is to be
proposed and exemplified in the chapters that follow

seeks to unite the principles underpinning both methods but as part of a newly conceptualised rationale for the teaching of writing in schools.

My own experience with 2G was traumatic because of the magnitude of the problems most of the pupils were facing and because of my own lack of experience, skill and knowledge as a teacher. The difficulties that large numbers of so-called 'average' or 'below average' children are facing may not be on so large a scale or as intense as pupils with severe learning problems like those in 2G, but they are none the less real and often difficult to solve. What follows will, I hope, enable teachers to offer more effective help in the teaching of writing no matter what their pupils' ages, achievements or abilities. My text therefore is not addressed only to teachers working with classes like 2G, small groups of pupils with serious learning difficulties who need to be given individual attention by a specialist teacher, but to those working in primary, middle and secondary schools teaching the mass of children and trying to help them to write more effectively.

My purpose in writing this book, then, is not to present definitive answers about the teaching of writing in schools, but to share with the reader my own increased understanding and insights about the nature of the writing process, which have been gained since those early experiences with 2G, and to offer a model of teaching which I believe to be coherent, sensitive to the individual differences among children, and more effective than the pragmatic fumblings towards success that I relied on earlier in my career. I hope that the exposition, illustration and discussion that follow will help others towards a better understanding of the problems experienced by their pupils when they are set a writing task, will encourage teachers to review critically their own classroom practice, and will contribute towards a more successful professional methodology in this domain.

The classroom rationale that is to be offered is, I believe, more structured and systematic than is at present the case in most schools and it undoubtedly demands much of teachers and pupils alike. But it is not impracticable, over-idealistic or needlessly complex; it has been developed in collaboration with a group of practising teachers and has been piloted and evaluated in their classrooms (Peacock and Roger 1984). Many other teachers are already working in their own ways towards the ideal that is to be presented. I hope therefore that what follows will help to clarify the thinking of these teachers

9

who are already sympathetic to my message and will offer them new insights and possible ways forward in their classroom teaching.

For those teachers who are more sceptical, I hope the book will challenge their thinking and encourage them to examine critically their own classroom practice. A more systematic approach to teaching need not be mechanistic or dehumanising, as some critics seem to assume, and I believe that if such an approach were to be given a greater chance of succeeding in the teaching of writing than has been the case in recent years, many children in our classrooms could benefit as a result. First, however, we seek to clarify the nature of the writing process itself.

Chapter Two

WRITING AND THE COMMUNICATION OF MEANING

To be an effective teacher of writing, you need to
be aware of the different kinds of demand writing
makes when a child attempts to create a meaningful
written text. Although in the course of in-service
work, teachers have often commented on how difficult
they find it to produce an extended written text
themselves, in comparison with their pupils they are
clearly skilled and experienced writers. The difficulties they face are more likely to be 'higher
order' problems of expression and organisation rather
than the 'basic' struggle to create the appropriate
marks on the page in order to convey a relatively
simple message.
      For adults most of the essential skills involved
in writing have been acquired in the distant past
and are easily taken for granted; they have become
part of their habitual, unreflecting behaviour. As
a result we tend to be unaware of the importance of
many aspects of the writing process and fail to
understand the problems that many of our pupils are
experiencing. It is easy to direct attention to the
most obvious surface features of a script (the handwriting, spelling and punctuation, for example), to
examine over-critically the subject-matter that is
being communicated, and to complain about the way
sentences and paragraphs have been constructed. We
ignore the successes that have been achieved by the
writer and fail to recognise or understand the difficulties a pupil is trying to overcome in the effort
to master the complexities of the writing process.
      This and the following chapter, therefore,
examine the nature of writing as a process of communication and analyse its constituent elements in
order to increase the reader's awareness of what
appears to happen when a child attempts to create a
written text. The chapters aim to provide an over-

view of the subject rather than an in-depth critical
study and although they draw on research from a wide
variety of sources, they explore the nature of the
writing process from the particular viewpoint of the
classroom teacher.

SPEECH AND WRITING

It is tempting to think of writing as being simply
speech written down and to encourage children to
make a direct link between what they say and what
they write. If reading is a 'kind of listening with
a visual rather than an aural input', (Roberts and
Lunzer 1968 p.220) then it may also be helpful to
think of writing as a 'kind of speaking' but with a
visual rather than an oral *output*. Writing and talking may be thought of as parallel language modes with
essential features in common.
    Both writing and talking are clearly productive
activities in the sense that they create language
outcomes just as reading and listening are both rec-
eptive activities. In talking, the meanings which a
speaker wishes to communicate are encoded and trans-
mitted as 'noises in the air' - the symbol system of
oral language - to be perceived and reinterpreted by
a listener. In much the same way a writer seeks to
communicate meaning to a reader but by means of the
visual symbols and conventions of written language
instead of the systems of sounds which characterise
speech. So it is possible at this very general level
to conceptualise writing as a 'kind of speaking'.
But, given this fundamental similarity, there are
also important differences between the two language
modes that we must be sensitive to if we are to understand the demands that face an inexperienced writer.
    Most children when they begin their primary
schooling are usually competent in their use of spoken
language - that is, they are reasonably proficient
speakers and listeners for the demands made on them
in their daily lives. If there were no crucial differences between the nature of speech and writing
beyond the learning of a new visual code to match the
symbols of speech, then any difficulties in writing
experienced by pupils in schools would be essentially
problems of transcription, that is, difficulties
associated with the transferring of a linguistic
message 'inside the head' of the writer on to the page
via the conventions of spelling, punctuation and
print. Considerable evidence now exists, however, to
show that this view is unacceptable. The differences
between speech and writing are often fundamental and

complex. Failure to master the conventions of writing should not be thought of as merely a failure in the ability to transcribe.

Writing is normally a continuing and sustained act of communication. This is not true of most spoken contexts especially those most commonly experienced by children. As speakers children are most accustomed to 'short burst' utterances and the give and take of interruptions, questioning and replies from their listener(s). Writing - even 'short burst' writing - is in contrast a more solitary and demanding activity. The writer normally seeks to maintain an independent and if possible uninterrupted flow of language sometimes over an extended period of time before the final written product is achieved. Compared to speech, too, writing is 'painfully slow' (Frank Smith 1982, p.22). In many face-to-face contexts children can generate speech with considerable speed, skill and fluency, but when they attempt to convey an extended sequence of meaning in writing, they discover that somehow they have to slow down their thought processes. In order to have time to make the necessary marks on the page they have to hold a unit of language in short-term memory and resist the temptation to allow their thoughts to race ahead. At best most children seem to achieve only an uneasy compromise between focusing on the immediate topic and thinking around and beyond it.

In most face-to-face encounters children collect and communicate their thoughts unselfconsciously. While generating language they are able to call upon a variety of supporting strategies which the listener accepts and which assist communication. They repeat themselves, get entangled in grammatical mazes, use 'filler' words, phrases, and noises - *you know, see, um* - in order to help them make social contact with their listeners and to provide an opportunity to continue to plan and generate a continuing sequence of utterances. Over and above such linguistic devices, like all speakers, they are accustomed to using the varied paralinguistic features of oral communication to emphasise, clarify and develop their meaning, using pitch and volume of voice, speed of delivery and intonation as well as facial expression, gesture and body movement.

For example, although the visual and oral dimensions of the scene are absent, the following short extract from a classroom lesson is clearly a transcript of spoken language, not a text intended from its outset for the medium of print. The boy in question is struggling to articulate his response to

the death of a cat which has been described in the
poem 'A Case of Murder' by Vernon Scannell. The
text has already been read in class and is being
discussed with the teacher:

> *It's a feeling of being squashed in the doorway*
> *makes you sick ... like a nut ... em, the way*
> *the poem, er, it compares the ... the being*
> *crushed ... like a nut ... makes you sick ...*
> (Slater 1981)

In contrast writing is normally much more organised
and coherent. The writer is expected to edit out
digressions and repetitions. In most written texts
there is no place for 'fillers' and only very limited
opportunities exist to communicate the subtleties of
intonation, facial expression and gesture (by means
of underlining, for example, exclamation marks or
block capitals). In fact in creating a written text
of any length the writer is normally expected to
choose language forms that are more concise than
those used in spoken contexts, but at the same time
expression is often more complex in its syntax and
more varied in its vocabulary.

In most spoken contexts children are accustomed
to sharing the same physical setting as their listen-
er(s); they can point directly to features of the
conversation and demonstrate aspects of their meaning without feeling a need to be fully explicit in
their language. They are accustomed to their listeners sharing the same understandings and assumptions
with experiences held in common so that precise
detail and explicitness are not normally necessary
features of communication. If the speaker should
fail to communicate effectively the listener can
interrupt and probe for more information.

Quite the opposite is true of most contexts for
writing. Normally the writer and reader do not share
the same physical setting. The fact that they do in
schools, where the skills of writing are learned,
tends to increase the writer's problems, as we shall
see later, rather than alleviate them. Nor can the
writer (outside the classroom) always rely on the
reader's acceptance of shared meanings and understandings. No reader is normally present to interrupt or demand more information; the written message
has to be made explicit and clear except in very
informal circumstances like the writing of a personal
letter.

By way of an example, the following piece of
writing by Andrew (aged 9 years), presented without

corrections but with names changed, demonstrates
that although the writer has a dramatic tale to
tell, he has experienced some difficulty in the
attempt to communicate his subject-matter in written
form. Although these difficulties are partly related
to the surface features of the final written product
- the title of the piece should, for example, be *A
Fight with the Reids* not *A Fit with the Reds* - more
importantly they can be related to his lack of an
intuitive understanding about the main differences
between spoken and written forms that have been discussed in the preceding paragraphs. Andrew does not
yet seem to have at his command language structures
that are appropriate to a written text. Yet the
reader is left in no doubt that the writer could
have given a very lively and effective oral account
of the event.

> ### A FIT WITH THE REDS
> *I was watching a fit with the Reds. And the
> Camerons and the polis and two of the Reds got
> poot in the polis van and they cict the vans
> door and my dad came in and I told my dad and
> he came out and a polis was going to hit one of
> the Reds and he movd at of the rod. And my mum
> got hit and my dad went to him and he punchet
> him and he fell down and my big bruther was out
> of the game be case he did not want him poot in
> jayl and my mum jumpt on a polismans back and
> the polismans hats where geting frowing* the
> hats abwte and at the end the polisman drone*
> away the Reds wer cicing about in the van.*

> **frowing - thrown   drone - drove*

These essential differences between the nature of
speech and writing, which have been summarised and
exemplified, are well documented elsewhere and should
by now be widely accepted. But the differences are
not absolute; they relate to abstract and stereotyped
representations of the writing and speaking processes.
In everyday contexts these stereotypes or models
soften and begin to blur according to the purpose
of the communication and its intended audience.
Most teachers are now prepared to accept that
no single correct form of English exists which is
suitable for every communicative purpose, context
and audience. The concept of 'correct' language
has given ground to that of 'appropriate' language
or a form of English which is appropriate to context,
purpose and audience. Teachers are much more sen-

sitive than was the case even in the recent past to the importance of different registers of language in different communicative settings; they are more willing to accept the strengths of different social and geographical accents and dialects.

The accepted forms of written English are less flexible and varied than those of speech, but there exists none the less a continuum from the most formal contexts for writing to the least formal depending on the purpose of the communication and its intended audience. A very personal letter to a close friend, for example, may possess many of the characteristics of spoken language while a public lecture may demonstrate many of the features of writing (and is sometimes simply a written text read aloud). The concept of a writer's *repertoire* should therefore be as important to the teacher of writing as it is in the teaching of spoken English. An essential professional aim is not simply to develop skills in writing, but to seek to develop a child's expertise and self-confidence as a writer so that he/she may become proficient in as many communicative contexts as possible.

CATEGORIES OF WRITING

Considerable work has been done in recent years to clarify and categorise different kinds of writing, undertaken in different contexts, for different purposes and audiences. The most widely known and probably the most influential in the school system is that developed by James Britton, using the terms *transactional, expressive* and *poetic* to categorise functions in writing (from the viewpoint of the writer) and categorising a pupil's perceived audience in writing on a continuum in terms of self, the teacher, a wider known and an unknown audience (Britton *et al* 1975). Other frameworks can be found, for example, in Cooper and Odell (1977), where the categories are based on a more traditional rhetorical framework, and in Applebee (1981) under the heading 'Uses of school writing'.

One of the problems associated with Britton's system of classification is that when you try to apply the system to the pupils' scripts (especially the function categories) you may find yourself involved in an emotive debate with colleagues as to which category a particular script may belong. This is because the system relates to the writer's perception of his/her task and audience rather than to the reader's perception of the written product

that is eventually created. The definitive answer
to any disagreement cannot exist within the script
itself; it will lie only within the head of the
writer. Consequently relevant data will almost
certainly be accessible only during or immediately
after writing, when the pupil concerned can be
questioned or is willing to report. However, a main
strength of Britton's system is that the central
category of expressive writing is one which throws a
bridge between the stereotypes of talking and writing
that were discussed in the previous section. The
language of expressive writing, like that of most
informal talk, is 'close to the self, verbalising
(the writer's) consciousness'; it is 'not highly
explicit' and is 'relatively unstructured' display-
ing the writer's close relationship with the reader.
The other main categories - transactional and poetic
- are likely to produce outcomes that are more formal,
explicit and deliberately organised.

Charles Cooper and Lee Odell, on the other hand,
specify different kinds of writing *product* and
include in their list dramatic writing, reporting,
generalising and theorising, research, personal
writing, poetry and prose fiction, and business/
practical (including technical reports, explaining
a process and giving instructions) (Cooper and
Odell 1977 p.x-xi). Arthur Applebee's categories
are developed from Britton's but are organised under
three general headings specifying *writing activities*.
The first set - *Informational Uses of Writing* -
includes note-taking, recording, reporting and
summarising, but also includes higher-level
activities such as theory, analysis and persuasion.
The second set - *Personal Uses of Writing* includes
personal letters and notes, and journal or diary
writing. And the third set - *Imaginative Uses of
Writing* - includes stories, poems and play scripts.

Applebee also introduces the additional
category *Writing Without Composing* which is glossed
as 'mechanical uses of writing'. This category
includes such classroom tasks as multiple-choice and
short-answer exercises, copying, dictation and
translation. His own research study, based partly
on extended observation in two American high schools,
indicated that although almost half of observed
lesson time involved some kind of writing activity,
these activities were dominated by 'mechanical' and
'informational' uses of writing (24% and 20% of
lesson time respectively) with informational writing
comprising in the main of note-taking. Only 3% of
observed lesson time was devoted to longer writing,

requiring students to produce at least a paragraph
of coherent text (Applebee 1981, pp.27-32).

These findings are similar to Ernest Spencer's
in his study of writing in a representative sample
of Scottish secondary schools (1983). Although he
found much variation in the amounts actually
written by individual pupils in different schools in
various categories of writings, *overall,* he con-
cluded, about half of what is written in school
appears to be copied or dictated and about one
quarter apparently consists of short answers (single
sentences or blank filling). The remaining quarter
is accounted for by continuous writing in the pupils'
own words, but more than half of this category seems
to be short (perhaps a few lines only per task).
Almost all continuous, extended, 'own words' writing
(that is, of more than one page in length) appeared
to be done in English, although even in this area,
in the week of the project's survey, 70% of the
pupils involved did not appear to write more than one
page of continuous writing in any task (Spencer 1983,
p.12).

It is on this field of extended 'own words'
writing where pupils struggle to communicate their
own meaning (apparently neglected in some classrooms)
that our own attention is focused.

THE TEACHING OF WRITING : A COGNITIVE APPROACH

The conceptualisation of the writing process itself
remains problematic. What cognitive processes are
involved when a pupil plans, drafts and revises a
classroom writing assignment? What 'skills' both
obvious and hidden must a pupil master to compose
and communicate a message in written form? There
are no simple, clear-cut answers to these questions,
but in the remainder of this chapter we introduce
and illustrate a model of the writing process which
is derived from information processing theory and
which is, I believe, coherent, convincing and helpful to the teacher of writing.

Carl Bereiter and Marlene Scardamalia have
identified three distinct approaches to the teaching of writing in schools, each based on different
assumptions about the nature of the writing process.
The two dominant classroom modes are identified as
the 'sub-skills' and 'holistic' approaches to writing,
which were discussed in the previous chapter. The
'sub-skills' approach is analytic; it accepts that
the writing process can be broken down into discrete,
identifiable elements and taught as separate skills.

The eventual goal of the approach is that these skills will be 're-assembled' in the course of a continuing programme of learning directed towards eventual total mastery of all forms of writing. The 'holistic' approach, on the other hand, assumes that all aspects of the writing process are inter-dependent; although relevant skills can be identified, none can be taught effectively in isolation. The total communicative context is of prime importance and given a supportive classroom environment pupils will develop appropriate skills intuitively and incidentally. Whereas the first approach - the sub-skills - accepts the importance of deliberate class-room teaching and planned goals, the second - the holistic - accepts the greater importance of pupils' development and 'growth' and gives the teacher a more delicate and self-effacing role. (Scardamalia *et al* 1981 Introd.)

The third overall strategy identified by Bereiter and Scardamalia is termed a 'cognitive' approach. This third approach seeks to reconcile the differences apparent in both earlier rationales. It is based on attempts to understand the cognitive processes which appear to go on in the act of writing and it accepts that these different process-es can be identified and made more effective as a result of explicit teaching. In this respect it accepts the principles of the sub-skills model, but a cognitive approach also recognises the importance of a *system* of inter-related skills. Whereas the sub-skills approach identifies separate elements of the writing process and seeks to teach them in isolation, the cognitive approach recognises that the relevant mental processes must function together as part of a system within a communicative context. Consequently teaching activities must seek to preserve the system intact (as in the holistic approach).

The mental processes involved in writing are awesome in their complexity. The more you reflect on the problem of what happens the more impressed you become that any child learns to write at all. For the classroom teacher struggling to give attention to the problems of (say) 30 children, it is essential to attempt to reduce this bewildering complexity to manageable proportions without oversimplifying to an unacceptable degree or trivialising the issues involved. This goal is achieved, I believe by accept-ing a model of writing derived from information-processing theory which helps us to distinguish the essential elements of the writing process more clearly and to understand better their inter-relation-ship.

Underpinning an information-processing model of human cognition is 'the cybernetic hypothesis' (see, for example, Galanter 1966, Chapter 9). According to this hypothesis the workings of a man-made information-processing system can be accepted as a metaphor for the workings of a human mind. By making the comparison, it is argued, we are helped to understand more clearly the cognitive processes which underlie human behaviour but which are not easily accessible to direct study or observation.

Fundamental to the model is the concept of 'feedback'. A 'feedback loop' conveys information from some kind of 'sensing device' to an active counterpart. The information received from this sensing device causes the active counterpart to carry out operations of some kind (or *not* to carry them out depending on the nature of the information received). The sensing device is therefore constantly gathering information and conveying it via the feedback loop to the active counterpart to initiate, if necessary, some kind of action. The sequence is one of constant testing to secure information, the intermittent relaying of information to the active device and intermittent activity as a result of the information received.

The testing or sensing device is entirely dependent on some kind of prior information or pre-programming; it has to 'know' what information it is required to search for. This essential prior information is represented as a 'plan' or 'script' and the sensing device constantly searches for 'congruence' or a state of affairs that matches the pre-arranged 'plan'. The 'plan' can be simple or complex depending on the need. If congruence exists, no action is required. But if the sensing device detects 'incongruity' between the original 'plan' and what is being tested, this essential information is conveyed to the active device by means of the feedback loop. Action then occurs to ensure that congruence with the 'plan' is brought about. The sequence, therefore, comprises a continuing cycle of testing, information processing and activity to ensure a stable match between the arranged 'plan' and the environment or system it is connected to.

An easily comprehended example of the model in practice is that of a thermostat controlling a central heating system in a house. The 'plan' is the heating level predetermined by the householder, the 'sensing device' is the thermostat which tests the environment to ascertain room temperature. If incongruity is sensed, however, and the temperature

drops below the required level, information is conveyed to the 'active device' - the boiler - which is
then brought into operation to increase the supply
of heat.

In this example the 'system' is relatively
simple and self-contained; the 'plan' comprises no
more than a pre-determined temperature. However,
the 'test-operate-test' sequence found in something
like a central heating system, with its 'feedback
loop', can also help us to gain a better understanding of a much more complex human activity like
writing. If we apply the test-operate-test sequence
to a child's struggle to communicate meaning by means
of written symbols, what kinds of 'test' will the
writer be likely to carry out? How will he/she
ascertain whether 'congruity' or 'incongruity' has
been achieved in the course of the 'operations' that
are involved in the act of writing?

The comparison with the working of a heating
system may seem to imply an unacceptable mechanistic
approach to human learning with a teacher seeking to
'programme' a pupil's responses in much the same way
that a householder programmes his/her heating system.
When, therefore, we attempt to compare both the
hidden processes and the visible evidence of human
cognitive activity with man-made mechanical paral-
lels, we must recognise the importance of three
essential differences.

First, an overall mental 'plan' or 'script'
that influences a sequence of co-ordinated human
activities (like writing) is not simple or self-
contained. Behaviour is complex; one cycle of
activities normally overlaps another and may interact
with it. Different cognitive 'plans' will relate to
and influence different kinds of related activity.
In the case of writing, for example, we have to
compose what we wish to write as well as create the
symbols which will communicate our message.

Second, although clearly all human beings are
normally subject to a variety of important social
influences (including that of the school), our mental
'plans' or 'scripts' are self-generated, not created
for us by others. As a result of our experiences as
we grow up and interact with others, we actively
construct and store increasingly complex networks of
meaning in visual, linguistic and kinaesthetic form,
which help us to organise and retrieve different
kinds of knowledge and experience. New understandings are constantly assimilated into these frameworks or schemata, or the frameworks themselves are
adapted in order to accommodate new ways of thinking.

21

The mental 'plans' that influence and direct our behaviour are therefore dynamic and flexible.

And third, unlike machines, the kinds of 'plans' we construct will be shaped by the influence of the values and attitudes we have acquired as individuals. Even if it were a desirable aim, the notion of teachers 'programming' their pupils in schools is impracticable. Children are clearly motivated by their own values and attitudes which 'modulate' their behaviour; their intentions in the classroom sometimes conflict with their teachers' objectives. In order to succeed, therefore, any approach to the teaching of writing must take account of this dynamic relationship between teacher and taught. Meanings and values about the nature of success in writing cannot be imposed; they need to be negotiated and exchanged so that children can gradually construct their own independent values for judging their success as writers.

If, then, we begin to apply the features of our prototype information-processing model (the 'test-operate-test' sequence and the 'feedback loop') specifically to the act of writing, we begin to understand more clearly the complex processes that appear to be involved. An experienced writer has already acquired important underlying values and attitudes about the nature of writing itself and the purposes of a particular intended communication. These are likely to influence the ways in which a writing task is perceived and approached. Once, though, the pen begins to move across the page (or the fingers start to strike the keyboard) directed by the mind of the writer, a complex continuing cycle is set in motion. The writer can be observed to pause and reflect, to create the symbols of the text, to pause again before continuing, and to review and emend what has been written. In the act of writing, we appear to be constantly engaged in an independent and complex process of testing and comparison. As we create the symbols on the page, we unwittingly seek to match different features of the text we are struggling to compose 'in our heads' and to construct in a visible, tangible form, with the different kinds of models and images that are stored and organised in our mental 'plans' for different kinds of writing. We intuitively draw on this accumulated knowledge and on our understanding of what will 'count' as appropriate writing for this particular context, purpose and audience. Although the communication of meaning may remain our essential aim as we write, there exists subsumed beneath this overriding purpose a complex amalgam of understandings and skills which as experienced writers we readily take for granted.

In the next chapter we explore this complex totality in greater detail and analyse its constituent elements in order to understand more fully the demands that are made on a beginning writer.

Chapter Three

THE WRITING PROCESS : AN ANALYSIS

Traditional thinking about the nature of the writing
process encourages us to think of writing as a
linear sequence of events. The writer begins by
planning and reflecting on his/her subject-matter,
then settles down to write; once the writing is
completed, he/she checks for errors, makes improvements to ensure greater clarity and readability, and
then completes a final fair copy. However, reflection quickly indicates that this linear sequence is
unsatisfactory. In the first place, it takes account
of extended 'own words' writing alone. Many classroom writing tasks, it appears, require only copying
from blackboard, textbook or teacher's dictation and
this kind of writing requires no phase of planning
or reflection. More importantly though, the notion
of the linear sequence in writing is an illusion, no
matter what the task. Feedback is not confined to
the final stage of checking and editing. There are
constant interruptions between each phase and constant movements back and forth between the phases
identified in the model as the writer proceeds towards his/her final goal. As indicated in the
previous chapter, the writer is constantly reflecting, making the marks on the page, checking, alter-
ing words and phrases or aspects of them, as the
written message develops.
        As an alternative, Donald E.P. Smith (1976
Chapter 3) presents a more convincing model of
writing derived from information-processing theory.
Whatever the input (words copied from a blackboard,
a paragraph dictated by the teacher, or silent
language composed 'in the head' of the individual
writer) information is conveyed to the 'receiving
system', is processed by the brain and translated by
means of the 'producing system' into written symbols
- the marks that appear on the page. Built into

this process is the notion of constant feedback which continuously influences and changes the nature of the developing activity in accordance with the 'plan' in the mind of the writer. As Smith indicates, writing presents special difficulties to the learner because processing is a 'cross-mode' task; writing normally involves the translation of what is *heard* (either the voice of the dictating teacher or the silent voice 'inside the writer's head') into what is *seen* (i.e. the symbols of print).

In this proposed model of the writing process, however, feedback seems to occur only as a result of the actual outcomes of the writer's internalised cognitive activity. We see what we have written (while we are engaged in the act of writing) and the 'sensing device' in our brains compares this outcome with the 'plans' and the 'images' that exist in our imaginations. If we detect 'congruity' between what has been written and our mental 'plans' we proceed with the task. If, however, we perceive 'incongruity' we cross out what we have written or make appropriate changes.

However, it is arguable that in extended 'own words' writing the sensing device also provides feedback *before* the writer produces the actual marks on the page as well as during the act of writing and after the completion of a task. In other words, we check for congruity while we are actually composing and rehearsing inside our heads the message we intend to convey via print or handwritten script. Consequently a more acceptable and comprehensive model of the writing process comprises the three inter-dependent stages of composing, transcribing and reviewing, with feedback represented as an essential and integral influence at each stage. (Frederiksen and Dominic 1981 p.68)

'Composing' involves the activities of planning and rehearsing the content of the message to be communicated in written form, of finding the appropriate words and grammatical structures; 'transcribing' involves the motor-skills of creating the actual symbols on the page by means of pen, pencil or keyboard and the command of orthographic conventions (such as spelling, punctuation and paragraphing); 'reviewing' involves the editorial skills of checking for errors, seeking improvements to the clarity of the message being conveyed, to the physical lay-out of the script and to style. Review 'feedback' is presented as a constant process affecting all stages of the act of writing from the reformulation of the composed message to the efforts to translate this message into a written text.

If we are to review effectively when we are engaged in a writing task, then it follows from previous discussion that we will need to have created appropriate cognitive 'plans' or 'scripts' to act as templates against which we can make judgements concerning congruity and incongruity while we compose and transcribe our written text. In composing, we need to possess internalised models of what will count as an acceptable word or phrase in a particular context, as an appropriate sentence structure or style of address for a perceived audience. When we transcribe, we also need internalised models for the shapes of words and the accepted conventions of written forms. The skills we need to develop in order to write with success do not exist in isolation. They are intrinsically related to the different kinds of internalised 'plans' for writing that we have constructed and to our values and intentions as writers.

Each of these three main areas - composing, transcribing, and reviewing - are now examined in greater detail, together with the different demands which are placed on us when we seek to process and give form to a message we wish to communicate as a written text.

COMPOSING

The term 'composition' when applied to classroom writing still tends to be interpreted by teachers as signifying the final written product, something that has already been 'composed', a script ready for the teacher to respond to and assess. By using the term 'composing' in this section we seek to focus attention instead on the internal processes of composition - what goes on 'inside the heads' of the pupils before they create or while they are creating the marks on the page that will actually constitute their written message. Composing a text in your head is not a distinct, separate activity that is the first part of a sequence connecting it to transcribing and then reviewing. The three activities are inter-related and inter-dependent. The writer constantly shifts backwards and forwards between the three activities, composing the text, creating the symbols on the page, and checking and reflecting upon what has been written. We can be formulating new subject-matter while we are actually writing the words of a previously composed text or reviewing what we have written.

The composing of a text can be particularly
difficult for beginning writers and as teachers we
need to be sensitive to the different kinds of
problems pupils are likely to be experiencing. The
different kinds of constraint that we need to negot-
iate and overcome when we struggle to compose a
text can be thought of under four headings; each
brings with it different problems. These four headings are related to the *cognitive* demands of composing a text, the *linguistic* demands made on us by the
subject-matter, and the demands of *context* and
communicative setting. (Frederiksen and Dominic
1981 p.19) The *cognitive* demands of composition are
apparent; in order to compose a message, we must have
'something to say'. We must be able to understand
the content of what is to be communicated, must be
able to recall it and organise it in an appropriate
way. If this is not the case, the act of composing
and expressing must at least help a writer *towards*
a better understanding or a more clearly organised
representation of his/her subject-matter. ('How
do I know what I think till I see what I write?').
There can be no precise distinction between the
cognitive and linguistic demands of writing, because
each aspect depends on the other. Composition does
not consist of two separate, independent parts -
ideas (thoughts, content) on the one hand, and
expression on the other - because 'meaning is made
manifest in its expression............As a manifest
reflection or consequence of anything in the mind,
idea and words must come into existence together'.
(Frank Smith 1982 p.195)
    The *linguistic* demands of composition are
probably underestimated in their complexity. It
is easy to recognise that the writer has to find the
'right' words and put them in an appropriate order,
but our present greater sensitivity to the differences between speech and writing indicate that
inexperienced writers cannot rely on their intuitive
knowledge of spoken language when they formulate a
message to be conveyed in written form (except perhaps for very informal purposes). Writers do not need
merely to exploit their 'language store' gathered
from prior experience of speech contexts. They must
understand how written discourse is put together,what
is involved in writing in different ways, what devices can be used to produce cohesion in the final
written product so that the text reads well and
'hangs together'. In fact, the successful writer
must develop a 'grapholect' appropriate to written
texts, just as he/she has developed at an earlier

age a 'dialect' (regional, social and personal) for
the purposes of spoken communication. The experienced
writer has at his/her command a range of written
registers for different purposes and contexts which
will be used intuitively and unreflectingly as the
occasion demands.

The nature of the language chosen to convey the
writer's meanings - the actual choice of words and
the sentence and paragraph structures - will depend
very much on what is appropriate to the *communicative
setting and context* of the writing. What kind of
writing is it? What is its purpose? What is the
register to be adopted? As indicated in an earlier
section we are now more sensitive to the importance
of different kinds of perceived audience in a child's
writing development.

The notion of audience is important on both the
affective and the cognitive dimensions of the
communicative context - that is, how the writer feels
and thinks about the intended audience for the
writing. A child perhaps needs to write for a 'warm'
and trusted adult who encourages and responds to
what is written, but any writer also needs to make
the necessary imaginative leap to understand (or at
least to hypothesise) what the audience for the
writing does or does not already know and understand.
Children in particular seem to experience considerable difficulty in deciding how much detail to include in their writing. They often leave out detail
that seems critical to the adult reader and they put
in detail that sometimes appears irrelevant.(Frank
Smith 1982 p.194)

The fact that classroom research in the United
Kingdom and North America has shown that the greater
part of school writing seems to be produced by
pupils for a teacher who is perceived in the role of
'examiner' to test the acquisition of subject-
specific knowledge is important in this respect.
(Britton *et al* 1975 p.137, Applebee 1981 p.94)
Pupils may intuitively recognise that there is little
need for them to make their final written message
explicit and clear, when they know that the teacher
who will read their scripts already possesses a
detailed understanding of the subject-matter. The
teacher will be able to predict, anticipate and read
'between the lines' as he/she reads what has been
written.

An essential problem for all writers to overcome
(but one that is especially difficult for young and
inexperienced writers) is our readiness to take for
granted the knowledge and understanding we ourselves

possess and our often unreasonable expectation that
our intended audience will share these meanings.
We assume that they will be willing and able to infer,
and predict (as is the case in most informal spoken
contexts between child and parent, sibling or friend).
This is why the classroom can often create underestimated difficulties for the inexperienced writer.
As indicated earlier a major advantage of writing
(as compared with speech) is that it enables us to
communicate some kind of message to a reader who
does *not* share with us the same physical environment
or experience. A written message therefore in most
contexts needs to be made explicit and clear. In
contrast, in schools children are often given
writing tasks which require them simply to convey
back information that has already been relayed to
them by their teachers. Pupils stoically accept,
as they are engaged in the task, that their teacher
is already fully apprised of the information they
are communicating.

   Contextual constraints, then, are of particular
importance in a school setting. The physical
environment of the classroom, including the presence
of the teacher and other pupils, may not be conducive
to planning and composing a piece of extended 'own
words' writing and frequently pupils have to overcome constraints of time, working to deadlines or
being interrupted by lesson bells and intervals.
Almost certainly the teacher will communicate to
the class explicit (and sometimes covert) rules about
the requirements of a particular writing task, what
is being looked for in the way of content, lay-out
and presentation of work. Pupils have to learn what
is required of them and how best to please their
teacher. In the secondary school in particular these
problems can become intense as pupils move from
classroom to classroom and from teacher to teacher.

   It is clear that viewed in this light, the
demands that need to be met by the inexperienced
writer when he/she seeks to compose a message are
daunting, even before a word is actually written.
In order to succeed, a writer has to make rapid (and
often unreflecting) decisions about what is appropriate to a particular task in each of the areas that
have been discussed. These decisions will depend
upon the purpose, context and audience of the
communication - what subject-matter to select, what
vocabulary and language structures to choose, and
how to organise the message that is to be conveyed.

   According to the theory of writing that has
been proposed, the only valid way in which such

decisions can be taken is for the writer to make use
of the notional 'sensing device', that we all
potentially possess, and attempt to match what is
being composed (either silently within the mind or
as the marks actually appear on the page) against a
set of internalised models. These models will represent what seem to us to count as appropriate
examples of written text when we complete tasks of
this kind. And our internalised models act as
templates against which we can match different aspects
of the text that we are creating.

A further deep-rooted problem may confront some
pupils in this whole field of composition which in
a sense brings together all the constraints that have
been discussed and is both cognitive and affective in
nature. In seeking to compose a text some children
may experience a fundamental conflict between the
sense of personal identity they are developing and
the requirements of the conventions of widely
accepted written forms. On the one hand, there is a
sense of being in control of your own knowledge and
language and getting satisfaction from communicating
a unique message, while, on the other, there is a
need to accept conventions, communicate successfully
to different kinds of audience and anticipate a
reader's expectations. This internal conflict may be
particularly acute for children whose spoken
dialects are widely divergent from standard written
forms and whose perceptions of life are markedly
different from the perceptions of the audience who
will read and respond to what they have written in
schools.(McLeod 1982 p.428)

TRANSCRIBING

Transcription is the process whereby the message that
has been formulated or composed is translated into
written form. In order to achieve this translation,
the message normally has first to be mentally rehearsed and held in short-term memory. Experienced
and successful writers will then make the necessary
marks on the page, normally using the conventions of
spelling, punctuation and textual lay-out without
reflection and having long ago mastered the motor-
skills necessary for a handwritten or keyboard text.

A source of possible difficulty may exist for
the beginning or inexperienced writer if the related
processes of composition and transcription both
demand equal attention. (Frank Smith 1982 p.120)
Ideally, the skills of written transcription should
be a set of automated, unreflecting sub-skills. If

the writer has to struggle to control movements of
the pen across the page, has constantly to pause over
details of spelling and punctuation, then clearly
attention and effort are likely to be diverted from
the processes of composition. Donald E.P. Smith
emphasises the importance of 'sub-routines' in
transcribing, or sequences of automatic, low-level
responses upon which are built more sophisticated
responses - for example the writing of letter-
strings, the unreflecting use of punctuation
signals, and of function and transition words. The
'over-learning' of such sub-routines are essential,
he argues, to the confident mastery of written
forms. (Donald E.P. Smith 1976 Vol.One p.85)
Aural dictation from a teacher or copying from blackboard or textbook may be helpful in this context.
These classroom strategies are acceptable methods of
developing fluency in transcription skills. An
insistence on children producing only extended, 'own
words' writing in the classroom may put an unreasonable processing load on the shoulders of some pupils
who are still struggling to master the skills of
transcription.

James Britton has drawn attention to the
importance of the amount of content or subject-matter
that can be held in focus in the mind at the time
of writing and we commented earlier on the marked
and inevitable differences in comparable speeds in
most contexts when we produce a written as opposed
to a spoken text. Clearly we can retain only a
limited number of words, or units of meaning, in our
head while we are actually writing and there may be
marked differences in this capacity between beginning and fluent writers. (Britton *et al* 1975 p.45)

For some people there may be very little mental
rehearsal of the words themselves before they are
actually written - the words 'just flow from the end
of the pen (if they flow at all)'. But mental rehearsal or 'self-dictation' may nevertheless be an
important initial transcription skill for the
beginning or unsuccessful writer:

> Often the writing and the inner speech appear
> to be concurrent; it is not clear whether we
> are 'reading' what we have written as we are
> writing or are writing to our own dictation.
> Perhaps any of the alternatives is possible
> and we switch from one to another, sometimes
> the hand leading the inner voice, sometimes
> the converse, and sometimes the two proceeding
> in tandem. And sometimes, for some people at

least, the composition can be entirely focused
on the hand alone, and there is no inner voice
at all.
                                    (Frank Smith 1982 p.105)

A child's lack of success in spelling can cause
considerable parental and professional anxiety.
Many teachers seem to accept that skills in spelling
will improve as a direct result of pupils reading
widely. After all, it seems convincing to argue
that children will somehow absorb the forms of words
as they read and that they will be able to recall
them when they in their turn create a written text
of some kind. And of course for some children this
is true. But there is no necessary correlation between success in reading and success in spelling.
The experience of wide voluntary reading does not
necessarily ensure that a child looks closely at the
structure of words, at recurring letter patterns or
develops an effective visual memory to ensure quick,
accurate recall. When reading with interest and
enjoyment it is possible for the child to recognise
whole words or groups of words and to be involved
totally in reconstructing the text's meaning.
     Margaret Peters has helped to clarify the
essence of spelling difficulties for the young or
unsuccessful writer. Whereas reading a text
involves the beginning reader in moving from the
unknown (the symbols or words on the page) via the
context (of, for example, a story) to the known
(that is, an understanding of the meanings involved),
the act of spelling in the creation of a written
text involves a process that is diametrically
opposed. The beginning writer has to move in this
case from the known to the unknown. That is, in the
course of composing a text the child has a grasp of
what he/she wants to say and may possess the appropriate language which is being silently rehearsed
'inside his/her head', but the actual forms of the
words in question may be unknown. The writer has
to try to visualise the words in question or 'sound
them out' and as a result can be faced by a variety
of possible combinations. There are clues in the
sounds of words, but in English these sounds may be
written or presented visually in many different ways.
(Peters 1967 pp.7-8)
     Similarly when teachers try to help to under-
stand the nature of punctuation, they often compare
the pauses a speaker makes between utterances in a
spoken context and similar pauses if a pupil's
written text were to be read aloud. 'Think where

32

you would pause', the argument goes, 'if you were
reading your story out loud and put in the punctuation at that point; commas for short pauses, full
stops for long pauses ...' But this advice is not
always as helpful to the beginning writer as it is
intended to be. The textual signals involved in
punctuation are *not* directly related to pauses in
most spoken contexts. In fact, a written text does
not have 'pauses' at all, unless it is written
specifically for recitation or performance. And
the analysis of examples of spoken language taken
from everyday speech contexts reveals that speakers
are likely to pause at a variety of different points
in any given utterance, and are often *unlikely* to
pause at the point where punctuation would occur if
the same, or similar text were to be written down.
(Doughty *et al* 1972 p.151)

The purpose of punctuation is not so much to
indicate to the reader pauses for 'breathing space'
as to help to act as a form of mediation between the
reader and the written text. Punctuation can help
to indicate some of the elements of emphasis and
intonation which a speaker is able to communicate
by means of paralinguistic features, such as volume,
pitch and facial expression, but, more importantly,
punctuation in a written text relates to the
structure of meaning. It provides 'a visible
spatial framework for the sense of what is being
said', helping the reader to grasp the logic of our
message and to see how our meanings are organised
and developed. (Frank Smith 1982 p.156)

Punctuation is to some extent a matter of
convention and personal preference, and to some
extent a matter of employing consistent rules, but
in order to punctuate effectively the writer needs
first to develop a confident intuitive grasp of the
logic that underpins the rules - the concept of a
sentence or paragraph, for example, or the logic of
the apostrophe - and all teachers of writing will
recognise how difficult many children seem to find
this. In addition though, writers must be able to
shift their own perspective and view the text they
are creating from the viewpoint of the reader. They
must be sensitive to providing the kinds of signals
that will help the reader to reconstruct the meanings of the written text. Again, ideally, as with
spelling, the use of these conventions has eventually
to be unreflecting and automatic so that we employ
them without reflection in the act of transcribing
or at a later stage during the phases of reviewing
or editing the text.

Finally, in order to transcribe successfully the writer must obviously possess skills in hand-writing (or keyboard skills) so that the essential marks that symbolise meanings can be made on the page. In order to do this pupils need to understand the nature of individual letters as well as possess skills in forming patterns of letters. They must develop a fluent, legible style of handwriting; and they must develop effective hand-eye co-ordination in the movement of the pen across the page from left to right, with appropriate movements and pressure of hand, fingers and wrist. (Jarman 1979 and Howell and Kaplan 1930 p.141)

The total demands, then, placed on the young or unsuccessful writer in the act of transcribing are considerable. Again the notion of feedback is important in our understanding of this dimension of writing. Transcription is not merely a motor activity which creates on paper a text that has been composed within the mind of the writer. Here, as with composing, we need to develop detailed and com-plex mental images or models for the principal features that have been discussed - the shapes of individual letters and the letter-strings that create a correctly spelled word, the visual lay-out of a text, the rules that underpin the signs that denote punctuation. As skilled writers we can sense incongruity as we create the necessary marks on the page and we act to bring about appropriate changes in the text often without being aware that the activity has taken place. We have developed appropriate psycho-motor skills that enable us to create the visual symbols or bring about the changes. In fact we intuitively accept that 'reviewing' is an essential and integral feature of the writing process not merely its concluding phase.

REVIEWING

A writer, then, rarely simply drafts a piece, checks it, then re-drafts it. In fact, it is helpful to distinguish three customary but different kinds of revision made by a writer to a written text - reviewing, revising, and editing. (Nold 1981)

The term 'reviewing' can be applied to the constant process of reflecting, checking and improv-ing while the writer actually makes the marks on the page or in the short pauses between bursts of writing. 'Revising', on the other hand, suggests a period of reflection when the written text is checked through by the writer, usually after a draft has been pro-

duced. The writer makes corrections to errors of
spelling and punctuation, seeks to improve the
clarity of the message that is being conveyed, and
to remove features that are perceived as being
clumsy or redundant in the way of style. 'Redrafting' would normally be applied to the process of
re-writing a piece, after critical revision has take
place, to produce an improved version, not merely a
'fair copy'. 'Editing' is the final stage where
the writer (or a third person with fresh perception)
checks for errors and perhaps reshapes content prior
to publication (whatever its form).

All four aspects of the reviewing or revising
process, however, share in common the critical
scrutiny of a written text to match its features
against a set of internalised models within the mind
of the reviser so that any incongruities can be
detected and resolved. This process of critical
examination may be carried out rapidly and unselfconsciously as we write, or at our leisure and with
a sense of greater detachment when a written draft
has been completed.

However, practising teachers may well observe
that in contrast unsuccessful writers do not
normally seem eager to review and edit their scripts
Mina Shaughnessy, for example, makes the following
apposite comment in her discussion of the teaching
of writing to older, low-achieving students:

> His (the writer's) movement is headlong, like
> someone making his way through a lush forest
> that closes behind him as he moves ahead. Any
> pattern that counters this pitch forward ...
> is likely to be avoided or mismanaged, and any
> behaviour that turns him back, as re-scanning,
> rewording, and proof-reading do, is against
> the grain and must be practised.
> (Shaughnessy 1977 p.80)

Despite this, it appears that the drafting and redrafting of a written text, critical review and
extensive editing are still fairly rare features of
classroom practice, even though their importance is
being increasingly accepted by teachers of writing.
(Applebee 1981 pp.83-84, Spencer 1983 p.38)

To conclude, then: in this and the preceding
chapter we have aimed to give the reader a concise
overview of the nature of the writing process,
placing the subject within the wider context of
communication by means of all four language modes.
This last chapter has in particular sought to

illuminate the principal demands made on a beginning
writer and the nature of some of the difficulties
that have to be overcome when a written text is
created. In the next and subsequent chapters we
begin to apply these insights to practical classroom
work and the problems teachers experience when they
try to help children to improve as writers.

Chapter Four

THE FORMATIVE ASSESSMENT OF WRITING

Some children do learn to write simply by writing.
However, as our opening chapter indicated, this may
be only a small proportion; not all children achieve
equal success or satisfaction in this field while
they are at school and many of them will give up
their struggle once they have left. They will write
as little and as rarely as circumstances permit.
What then can teachers do to help those pupils, who
do not learn quickly and easily, to master 'essential
skills' in writing and develop their self-confidence
as learners before possibly it is too late?
     The model of writing derived from information-
processing theory which was presented and discussed
in the previous chapters helps us to understand more
clearly the demands that are placed on beginning
writers as they struggle to communicate even a
relatively simple, but unique, message in writing.
In comparison the cognitive 'plans' of an experienced
writer are much more complex, consisting as they do
of networks of inter-locking 'sub-plans' related to
the activities of composing and transcribing a
written text. Many of the so-called 'essential
skills' of writing are so familiar to us that we
readily take them for granted because they are
directly related to our network of accepted internalised 'plans' and are derived from them.
     Clearly, the more we write, the more detailed
and complex our 'plans' should become and the more
confident our resulting skills. For most of us writing
can be described as a 'problem-solving activity'; we
have to overcome problems as we articulate our meaning in a written text, trying to find appropriate
words and language structures to suit the context,
the purpose and audience of the communication, and
to respect the graphological conventions that most
readers will expect. Many children will also be

struggling to master the psycho-motor skills that are essential to the creation of the actual symbols on the page. Inevitably, in attempting to complete a task, we are faced with sets of different kinds of problems which we must try to solve.

In one sense, of course, all children do need to learn to write by actually writing because those aspects of the writing process that must be 'over-learned' and become habitual unreflecting responses can only be acquired by constant practice. Some children in addition teach themselves how to develop their writing skills and learn intuitively 'on the job'. The 'sensing devices' they possess work well for them. They are alert to what they read, they can notice and recall the differences in vocabulary, tone and register they find in different kinds of texts; they learn to spell quickly and easily and they experience no serious difficulties in mastering the skills of handwriting. From an early age teachers can recognise that they are well on the way to becoming successful writers.

If most children did learn to write simply as a result of practice and intuitive insight, then our role as teachers would be comparatively simple. It would be that of encourager, motivator and incidental helper, a role that was rejected as being only partially satisfactory in our opening chapter. However, before we consider what teachers can actually do to help children to improve as writers, let us first examine a text written by Kevin, a pupil in his third year at secondary school. The purpose of the analysis is, first, to make connections between the theoretical discussion of the previous chapters and the problems being experienced by one individual writer, and, second, to prepare the way for a detailed consideration of a teacher's classroom role when he/she identifies strengths and weaknesses in a pupil's script and tries to help the writer to develop and improve.

KEVIN'S DIFFICULTIES: 'LET'S PLAY POISON'

First read carefully the handwritten text of Kevin's story which is presented as Figure 4.1. The piece was written as a classroom task after the teacher had read and discussed with the whole class Ray Bradbury's story 'Let's Play Poison'. In the original story an unpopular teacher is teased and tormented by a group of children both inside school and at home. Eventually one night he pursues them out of the house and falls to his death in an

Let play poisum

It was my Craig third year class the the Children didn't like hem. becouse he hands out puschment excise. for no orkason like talkeingor makeing noisray So the Children work out a plan to catch the teacher pet. His Name Was Roger mhine, sowe had to se Vjenser on anir English teache Roger play schess with the chess-group and our Mr craig some time ploys two So we invtend a gome colled poisen there Was 3 boys sixand 3 girls six of us. All togeth So we made our plan to get Roger We though him out of the window an cteacher askedhere he was Roger haid a broken leg and dan dnd teache seen up throw him out the police wus colled in nothexg happend ther mister crag left for good but one doy a teacher was off and mr Craig was very shakey sr and he was just the same but we treiment him and one night swhe skahe his top on his window and he kame and schesed but somtheig happend -next morning the clear wert in and crciod in the in ?

Figure 4.1 Kevin's Script: 'Let's Play Poison'

excavation trench while he chases the children in
the dark. The title of the story refers to a game
of dare the children play. The class were required
to write their own story using Bradbury's as a
springboard for their own ideas.

First impressions made by Kevin's script are
not good. The handwriting appears laboured and
uncontrolled and there are obvious spelling errors.
Some of these errors are trivial but others inter-
fere with the process of communication,making the
reader's task of interpretation more difficult. For
example, the first two words in line 3 should read
punishment exercises and there are also some distract-
ing omissions (the final *s* in several words, for
instance) and logical confusions (as with *two* for *too*
in line 8). There are difficulties also because the
punctuation is erratic or confusing; in the opening lines, for example, there is no punctuation
after *class* in line 1 and what appears to be an
unnecessary full-stop after *him* in line 2. More
importantly, though, the reader has to struggle to
reconstruct the meaning that the writer is seeking
to communicate. As an aid to comprehension, the
following transcript is provided, with words in
brackets indicating a possible reconstruction of the
writer's intentions:

LET'S PLAY POISON

*It was Mr Craig third year class the children
didn't like him because he hands out (punishment
exercises) for no reason like talking or making
nois(es) so the children work out a plan to
catch the teacher pet. His name was Roger
(Milne) so we had to (get vengeance) on our
English teacher. Roger play chess with the
chess group and our Mr Craig some time plays
two so we (invented) a game called poisen there
was 3 boys and 3 girls six of us all together.
So we made our plan to get roger. We (threw)
him out of the window an(d) teacher asked
(where) he was Roger had a broken leg and (arm)
and (a teacher had) seen us throw him out the
police was called in notheing happened then
mister Craig left for good but one day a teacher
was off and Mr Craig was very shakey and he was
just the same but we (tormented) him and one
night we shake (the top of his window) and he
came and chased (us) but something happened -
next morning the (cleaner) went in and (cried
'Any one in?')*

40

The writer is clearly experiencing problems in simply transcribing the message he wants to communicate. Some of these difficulties have already been noted and they would be apparent to most teachers of writing. In particular Kevin seems to be trying to represent the sounds of the words, which he 'hears' inside his head in the process of self-dictation, by equivalent phonic visual symbols in his script - *ge* for *get*, for example, *cl-ar* for *cleaner* and possibly the omission of the final *s* sounds as in *Mr Craig third year class*.

Some adults, some teachers even, might respond to what Kevin has written in a negative way, concentrating on the surface features of his script and emphasising his problems and what he has failed to achieve. However, those who work with slower-learning and low-achieving adolescent pupils like Kevin will recognise how difficult it is to persuade them to write at length at all and how easily their self-confidence as learners is destroyed. Many teachers who have responded to Kevin's script in discussion rightly indicate that he has in fact written quite a lot and that this may be a major achievement for him; he has an effective story to tell and the narrative is dramatic. There is, in particular, a successful note of concluding suspense as the cleaner arrives to find the house empty and the reader is left to infer Mr Craig's fate.

There is always a temptation, of course, for us to bring to a pupil's script our own cognitive 'plans' for writing and to infer qualities in the script as a result. Children often seem to be surprised and amused by what some adults find in their written work that was not part of their original intentions. In fact, many of the successful features perceived by adult readers in Kevin's script are derived (but not copied) from the original story by Ray Bradbury, including the ending.

Few teachers, on the other hand, have commented in discussion on Kevin's possible problems in composing his text and the difficulties that have been created because his story has been written in a classroom context with his teacher (and possibly his peers) as its audience. Kevin has read Bradbury's story (or has heard the teacher read it to the class) and he recognises that his teacher and peers are familiar with it. If this knowledge of Bradbury's text is shared, readers can anticipate and predict what is intended; they can read between and beyond the lines and can follow more readily the development of Kevin's story. In such circumstances does Kevin

need to make his narrative clearer and more explicit?
    Although it is difficult to claim that Kevin
has been completely successful in achieving a
register appropriate to a written narrative involving violence and suspense, his style does not lack
complexity. An attempt is made to link the main
ideas as they develop ('because...' 'so...' 'but
...') and sentence structures are not simple. However, there seems to be one fundamental problem
experienced by the writer when he composed the text
which teachers rarely allude to in discussion.
Kevin may be able to 'see' his story-line clearly,
but he experiences much greater difficulty in communicating it by means of language. In other words, he
may be able to encode his narrative visually as in a
film, but he finds it much more difficult to break
down these whole units of visual meaning into
comparable linguistic units. For example, Kevin can
depict in his imagination the sequence of events in
his story that begins with Roger being thrown from
the window and ends with the arrival of the police,
but he experiences difficulty when he tries to
convey the development of this sequence in words.
Too much information is confined in too little
space; the sequence needs to be 'unpacked' with much
more explanatory detail.
    An analysis of Kevin's story illustrates some
of the features of the composing and transcribing
processes in writing which were presented in the
previous chapter. It also helps us to identify some
of the strengths and weaknesses of his script and to
infer some of his difficulties as a writer. No
experienced teacher, of course, would suggest that
Kevin should be provided with a detailed list of all
his errors and shortcomings. This approach to his
work would be certain to undermine his self-confidence
and would probably be of little help to his development as a writer (or, I imagine, to his relationship
with his teacher). How, though, can we as teachers
help pupils like Kevin and many others whose problems
are less acute to improve?

THE NATURE OF FORMATIVE ASSESSMENT

Traditionally assessment in schools has always been
synonymous with evaluation. Marks, grades and
written comments on children's scripts have conveyed
the teacher's judgement about how well the pupil has
performed in completing the task that has been set.
Teachers also often use a form of short-hand abbrev-
iation in the margin of a pupil's text to point out

where the writer has made mistakes. In drawing
attentions to these 'corrections' teachers tend to
concentrate on surface features like accuracy of
spelling and punctuation and aspects of grammatical
structure. A concluding comment is also usually
added by the teacher (again often in abbreviated
form) to communicate encouragement or to indicate
the teacher's response to what has been written.
(McAlpine 1982, Spencer 1983 pp.35-36)

Formative assessment on the other hand represents a more systematic attempt on the teacher's
part both to identify strengths and weaknesses in a
writer's script and to help the pupil to overcome
selected difficulties. Although the term itself is
recent, formative assessment has in a sense always
been an essential part of good teaching practice.
Teachers recognise this and for most it is a
principal source of satisfaction in their work in
the classroom, because they see formative assessment
as being an important strategy for helping children
to develop as learners.

Formative assessment is not restricted to pupils'
written work nor does it relate to specific classroom
contexts; it is part and parcel of most daily teaching and learning encounters. Teachers are constantly
picking up a wide variety of 'signals' from their
pupils' behaviour, noticing what they say and do both
within and beyond the classroom. They store this
information 'in their heads' so that as a school
session progresses they gradually build up a detailed
bank of information about the individuals they teach
and upon which they can draw when the need arises.
Even in a traditional expository lesson with the
whole class, for example, different responses from
pupils to the teacher's questions can reveal
strengths and weaknesses in knowledge and understanding which can be used to the benefit of an individual
and sometimes of the whole class.

Normally, though, formative assessment is
associated with the interaction between the teacher
and a small group of pupils and most typically
between the teacher and a single individual. The
formative assessment of writing can take place either
while pupils are actually engaged on a writing task
or when a draft has been completed prior to redrafting. If, however, assessment is directed towards a
piece of completed work and the task is finished,
then assessment is clearly *summative* - the final
evaluation - not *formative* where assessment is
designed to improve work and help the writer to
develop further.

Success in the formative assessment of writing will depend partly upon the understandings teachers bring to the task of analysis when they read and respond to a pupil's script, partly on their ability to communicate their perceptions to the writer, and partly on their professional skills in helping pupils to overcome the difficulties they have identified. The discussion in the previous chapter was designed to help teachers to achieve a better understanding of the complexities of the writing process so that they can bring new insights to what children have achieved as writers and to the difficulties they may still be experiencing. What follows aims to assist teachers to develop their professional skills in the classroom so that they can communicate more effective formative advice to their pupils and help them to overcome some of the difficulties they have identified.

The processes of formative assessment can only begin to work when there is some kind of writing product for teachers to respond to. Consequently it follows that teachers can intervene to help individual pupils only when they are actually engaged on a writing task in the classroom or after a written draft has been completed. As regards the first approach - helping children while they are actually involved in the process of writing - teachers appear to differ in their beliefs and practices. At one end of a professional continuum teachers believe it is important to allow children an uninterrupted space of time so that they can write in silence while the teacher is occupied with a different (or even the same) task. In much the same way many children seem to dislike the presence of the teacher hovering in the background or peering over their shoulders as they write. At the other end of the continuum some teachers believe that it is important to move round the class, once a task has been set, not merely to maintain effective control and ensure that work has actually begun, but to be on hand to give advice and to solve individual problems as they arise.

My own experience in the course of working with teachers and as a classroom teacher myself suggests that the goal of achieving silent concentration and sustained endeavour in the classroom when working with mixed-ability classes and especially with slower-learning pupils is probably unrealistic. It is likely that pupils themselves will seek help both from their peers and from the teacher. Sometimes this call for help will be related to the nature of

the task set and how to respond to it and sometimes
to problems of detail while working on their own
scripts. Most teachers, I suspect, are likely to
accept these interruptions during 'silent' writing
and will try to help pupils overcome difficulties.
Sometimes, too, problems encountered with an
individual or group are developed as teaching points
for the whole class or simply relayed to everyone if
the teacher thinks the problem is important enough.

However, given the demands on the teacher's
time in the classroom it is probably unrealistic to
attempt any in-depth assessment while pupils are
actually writing their first drafts. Apart from
responding to specific requests for help and seeking
to monitor superficially the progress of the whole
class, teachers are likely to focus their attention
during this initial period of work on the most
obvious surface features of pupils' writing such as
lay-out, spelling and punctuation errors, and handwriting, or simply checking that the task has
actually been started by everyone.

The following classroom extracts, for example,
show a teacher providing some of these different
kinds of help while pupils are engaged in writing
their first drafts. The first example deals with
the layout of a drama script the main principles of
which have already been explained to the whole class
and exemplified on the blackboard. Here the teacher
explains to a pupil why extended stage directions in
the main body of the text should be separated from
the actors' dialogue:

Teacher   *... your stage direction wouldn't go on
the line, it would go underneath. Do you
want to look at a copy of the play so you
can see that? I'll get that for you.*
... (teacher reads a piece from the pupil's
text) *You have to have a stage direction
here.* (Reads) *And again this would go
underneath, otherwise the actor would be
tempted to read that. So it just makes it
easier to read ...*

Teacher   *Right ...*(reads script) *Question mark would
have to come in there because it's after a
question ... and again that's a question*
(Teacher fills in question marks)*... That
should have a capital of course because
it's the beginning of a sentence ...*

In the concluding example she relays advice to the whole class, interrupting their writing after identifying a problem in an individual script. Her advice refers to the importance of the narrative of the scene being communicated by means of the words and actions of the characters and is related to a recent experience the class had had of a visit to the theatre:

Teacher *... most of you have got your story-line pretty well shaped out. One or two of you have a bit of bother scripting it ... Most of you have been to the theatre, you've seen what it looks like, the fact that you've got to hear what's going on. You can't have your audience not being told what's happening; the actors have to tell some way or other either by their actions or by their speeches what's taking place. So make sure your actors tell the story ...*
                     (Peacock and Roger 1984 pp.51-52)

The teacher's comments in this context are understandably normally brief and to the point, and in the final extract she exploits an opportunity created by one pupil's observed difficulty to convey a general teaching point to the whole class. On the other hand, more thorough and detailed help can be given to pupils once their first drafts have been completed and before a second improved draft is attempted. Two broad approaches already exist for achieving this and both possess advantages and disadvantages for both teacher and pupil. The first is an oral interview or 'conference' between teacher and pupil; the second is more impersonal and remote and can be termed the 'postal' method.

A teacher-pupil conference is normally organised in a classroom setting during lesson-time at the teacher's or the pupil's desk and the conference comprises the teacher and either a single pupil or a small group. The analysis and advice that are offered, therefore, are not necessarily teacher-directed and dominated. The oral dimension of the encounter is an important feature of this approach, but the oral input need not take the form of a teacher monologue.

The 'postal' method, on the other hand, involves the teacher in taking away a batch of scripts for assessment and providing written comments concerning the strengths and weaknesses of each individual's work together with advice for improvements. These comments are written during non-teaching time in the classroom or staff-room or at home. Both the scripts and the written comments are then returned to the pupils in the normal classroom setting and when work resumes on a second draft pupils use the teacher's written comments as a guideline for developing and improving their drafts. In its most extreme form this method provides no oral support at all from the teacher for pupils, although random and incidental support can be provided when scripts are returned to individual children.

These two broad approaches can also be exemplified from recorded or observed classroom work. The first two examples are taken from different teacher-pupil conferences. In each case the (same) teacher begins by asking the pupils to read aloud the description of a character each has drafted as part of a unit of classroom work exploring the theme 'Witnesses'. As they read, the teacher follows their texts closely, frequently interrupting to ask questions. In the first extract the teacher is concerned with punctuation and especially with sentence structure but in the second he is clearly trying to tease out meaning and to help the writer to recognise a possible ambiguity in his text:

> *... But these are supposed to be sentences, so you need ... 'Mr McLean is aged ...' and you've got a full stop there, you need a capital there, right? ... You've got one, two three, four pieces of information there. You've got one, two, three sentences, but you can have the three because of this word here, which joins these two bits of information.*
>
> *So using that as a model go and see whether you can make any changes to other bits, and then bring it back to me again...*
> **********

Teacher	*That is used to show that there's shouting going on ... Young youths?*
Pupil	*A young youth, aye.*
Teacher	*Just a youth, I think.*
	'Stopped, looked up and ran away round the corner.'
Pupil	*Is there a 'd' in there somewhere?*
Teacher	*Well, I was going to ask you to look it up, but, yes, that's what's wrong.*
	Read this to me, ... 'He ... '

Pupil   *'He had black, hair, had black hair, wearing,
           ... wearing boots, black boots. He had
           an earring, earring ...'*

Teacher *What you've actually written is he had black
           hair and the black hair was wearing ...*

Pupil   *Ah*

Teacher *Right? Actually it reads not too badly ...
           because you know what you meant, but read-
           ing it off the page it's not clear, so:
           'He had black hair ...', that's one piece
           of information, '... was ... and he ...',
           what's wrong with that, can you tell me?*

(Peacock and Roger 1984 p.54)

These short extracts convey the impression of a purposeful teacher at work and a salient feature of his teaching style when providing help and support to pupils in the classroom was his systematic monitoring of the progress of the whole class together with short, intensive discussions with each pupil. These discussions themselves often (as in the first example) provided further goals towards which the writer could work.

Alternatively an example of a profile sheet used by a different teacher who was adopting the 'postal approach' to formative assessment is given in Figure 4.2. The sheet is organised under specific headings which are appropriate to a variety of writing tasks and, in addition to spaces for the teacher's comments and suggestions for improvements, there is a section for the writer to respond in turn if he/she so wishes. The use of this profile sheet is elaborated and illustrated in later chapters.

It is of course possible for teachers to exploit both of these broad approaches to the formative assessment of writing and to combine them so that the 'postal' report becomes the starting-point for individual discussion. Many teachers are already making use of both methods, though probably in less structured and elaborate forms than those described. There are clear advantages and disadvantages associated with each approach. The conference between teacher and pupil, for example, has the advantage of the immediacy of personal contact and flexibility so that aspects of a script can be taken up and discussed with the writer in some detail. But there are important disadvantages too which will be recognised by practising classroom teachers. The conference is very demanding of the teacher's time because you are working intensively with only a single individual or small group. It can be

Figure 4.2   Profile for Assessment

Name: ....

Date: ....

Writing task: ....   Draft Number: ....

	Teacher's Comments	Work for next draft	Pupil's Questions/Comments
SUBJECT			
POINT OF VIEW			
REGISTER			
ORGANISATION			
MECHANICS			

49

delicate too in terms of inter-personal relationships because the teacher may have to tease points out of discussion and be sensitive to the feelings of the writer whose work is being discussed. And the approach is difficult to organise and manage in a normal classroom setting because of the differing calls on the teacher's attention.

In contrast the 'postal' approach is more impersonal and remote than the conference, and it is more superficial, but it can in some ways make more effective use of the teacher's time. It is easier to organise and manage than the conference and it helps the teacher to gain a rapid overview of the work and progress of a whole class. The method ensures also that all children receive at least some feedback from the teacher about their work even if the amount of detail offered is necessarily limited.

IDENTIFYING STRENGTHS AND WEAKNESSES

In the earlier discussion of Kevin's script ('Let's Play Poison') we indicated how easy it is for teachers to be negative and destructive in their responses to and comments about a pupil's work. If this is the case, what kind of feedback should be offered to children, whichever approach to formative assessment the teacher adopts? Is there an appropriate sequence or pattern of events to follow or are there priorities which must be covered? Unfortunately there are no clear, definitive answers to these questions. The encouragement and advice which the teacher provides will depend on the nature of the writing task and the teacher's purposes in setting it, the individual pupil whose work is being discussed and the teacher's own preferred teaching style. However, some important and helpful generalisations can be made none the less.

The starting point for formative assessment should be positive. In other words, the teacher's first responsibility in providing feedback to the pupil should be to encourage and reinforce the success that a writer has already achieved. As in Kevin's case, it should always be possible for the teacher to find aspects of a pupil's script that can be encouraged and 'rewarded'. However, few first drafts (from any source) ever reach the point where improvement of any kind is impossible and the teacher's second essential responsibility should be to identify those aspects of the script (or a selection of aspects) which require changes and

development of some kind and to make suggestions
about how the draft can be improved.

Most teachers will accept that pupils should
not be overwhelmed by too many suggestions for making
improvements to their work. Teachers need to concentrate on selected difficulties only that are
thought to be the most important. As one experienced
teacher commented in interview:

> *It completely disheartens somebody who has*
> *continual marks under their words in something*
> *that they write. I would look at the work and*
> *I would think, 'What is the worst bit about it*
> *that needs to be corrected?' It wouldn't be*
> *the same approach all the time; it would depend*
> *on what they were handing me ...*
> (Peacock and Roger 1984 p.22)

Evidence from the same group of interviews carried
out with experienced teachers in three secondary
schools indicates that the criteria this particular
group of teachers uses to identify success in the
assessment of writing can be organised under the
following general headings, though not necessarily
in this order of importance. In their collective
judgement a written script should demonstrate:

- readily accessible meaning
- coherent structure and organisation
- choice of register that is appropriate to
  purpose and audience
- mastery of sentence forms and variety in
  sentence construction
- varied vocabulary
- respect for the conventions of spelling and
  punctuation (though not a demand for total
  accuracy)
- legible presentation
  (Peacock and Roger 1984 p.29)

However, in a formative discussion between teacher
and pupil these abstractions have to be made meaningful for the child and be applied to concrete
examples from the pupil's own writing. Almost
inevitably in seeking to do this teachers will
encounter problems of communication and understanding.

In the previous chapter when we explored the
central importance of a 'feedback loop' in the
writing process, it was hypothesised that a 'sensing
device' in the writer's mind seeks to match either

what is composed 'silently' in the head or is
actually written on the page, to a complex cognitive
'plan' of what counts in this context as appropriate
writing. Different kinds of overlapping 'plans'
exist for different kinds of writing according to
the context and purpose of the communication. When
the sensing device perceives incongruity between
the intentions in the mind of the writer or the marks
made on the page, on the one hand, and the cognitive
'plan', on the other, action is intuitively initiated
by the writer in order to bring about greater
congruity. How, then, can we relate this model of
the writing process to the formative assessment of
pupils' writing products in the classroom?

Clearly the notion of feedback is central to
both the writing process and formative assessment.
Skilled and experienced writers however, are
normally autonomous in the judgements they make.
Although help and advice from others may be available and given, generally speaking the feedback loop
functions as part of the writer's own independent,
intuitive behaviour. In contrast the aim of formative assessment in school is that feedback should be
directed from the teacher to the pupil/writer once
a draft has been completed. This is not to say that
a child working in a classroom does not operate
independently as a writer or is not motivated by his/
her own intentions and purposes when working on a
writing task. This can clearly be the case. But
the function of formative assessment in the classroom is for the teacher to intervene in this
process in order to help make the writer's success
explicit and to attempt to promote further development. On occasions in the classroom there may well
exist a mismatch of purposes and intentions, or mis-
understandings between teacher and writer. Most
especially a mismatch will almost certainly exist
between the complex cognitive 'plans' that teachers
bring to a writing task (evidenced by the quoted
general criteria for success adopted by a group of
teachers) when they respond to a pupil's draft and
the much simpler 'plans' that are likely to exist
in the mind of the beginning writer who has produced
it.

When as teachers we respond to a pupil's written
draft and we consider the strengths and weaknesses
of the script, we become aware of some of the
relevant aspects of our intuitive internalised
'plans' for the task, but many aspects we may readily
overlook or take for granted. Our response too is
likely to be influenced by the nature of the task

and our purposes in setting it, and also by our knowledge of the individual children who have written the different pieces - their past achievements as writers, for example, and possibly aspects of their personalities and behaviour as well. Judgements are made and advice is given in accordance with the qualities or criteria that 'float' to the surface of our minds. (Rowntree 1977 p.82)

From the teacher's point of view this strategy for formative assessment is not problematic. The task is set, the first drafts are written, and the teacher responds with encouragement, advice and practical help. For many pupils, though, this sequence of events may be a frustrating experience. If your teacher is to intervene to assess your script once the first draft has been written, how do you anticipate what is going to count as success? To a certain extent pupils are helped by their past experiences as learners and their understanding of the covert rules of the classroom. They will accept, for example, from prior knowledge that teachers of writing generally seem to expect certain features in a written product and in their first weeks with a new teacher they will learn that this particular individual has special likes and dislikes. None the less the formative assessment of writing may remain for many children the occasion on which they find out how well they have done. Preparing for this evaluation is perceived as a kind of guessing game which some pupils are more proficient in than others.

Formative assessment, then, should not be thought of as a self-contained phase in the lesson, but as one important part in a total sequence of the teaching of writing. To help children to obtain maximum benefit from the teacher's encouragement and help after a draft has been written, it is important to make a clear and explicit connection between formative assessment and the pre-writing stage. Such a connection (which is explored in detail in the next chapter) helps to clarify the nature of the task to be completed, and makes explicit what will eventually 'count' as success in the completion of the task. In other words, formative assessment needs to be intrinsically related to the pre-writing phase when the task is first introduced to the class by the teacher.

MANAGING FORMATIVE ASSESSMENT IN THE CLASSROOM

Most teachers in primary and middle schools should experience few difficulties in organising and managing a writing conference in the classroom either with an individual child or with a small group of pupils. Teachers in secondary schools, however, where classroom organisation tends to be less flexible, may find it more problematic. In the primary school, for example, teachers already spend an important part of their professional time in providing similar formative help for their pupils in the development of skills in reading.

In her summary of the results of extensive research in primary schools, which involved classroom observation and teachers' own logs of their classroom practice, Vera Southgate states that in most reading and writing periods teachers were seen to continually switch their attention from one child or group to another. And most teachers clearly worked hard to sustain this supportive activity. But, it is important to reflect that although a predominant activity in this observed work in primary schools was the teacher listening to individual children reading aloud, the act of listening was not always accompanied by much detailed instruction. And even though most teachers spent about forty minutes per day on this activity, because of constant and continuing interruptions and distractions of various kinds in the classroom, the actual amount of undivided attention any single child could expect was only very small.(Southgate *et al* 1981 p.147) Under such circumstances it is not surprising that teachers often appear (as in earlier examples of teachers working with individual pupils) to be directive rather than discursive in their approach to formative assessment.

In the field of writing many teachers in both primary and secondary schools appear to work in a similar manner. The whole class is treated as a unit when a writing task is set up and then teachers work with as many individuals as time allows during the lesson. Again, two interviewed teachers comment on their own classroom practice:

> *We do a general lesson with the whole class and*
> *I set them writing to do. When they're*
> *finished I call them out and advise them how*
> *to get their second draft better, usually on*
> *a one-to-one basis ... I usually manage to see*
> *everybody in the class maybe once a week, twice*
> *a week at the most ...*

> *You have to organise the classroom so that the*
> *bulk of the group carry on with some work that*
> *they can undertake independently without you*
> *being constantly interrupted while you're*
> *trying to deal with one particular problem...*
>
> (Roger 1982a)

The problems involved in organising and managing
individual help in the classroom when teaching
writing are clearly complex and demanding. If
teachers feel that they have not yet satisfactorily
solved these problems, or if they wish to make more
effective use of the time available to them in the
classroom for the purposes of formative assessment,
the following advice is offered. It is derived
from a variety of sources - from teachers' own
accounts of their professional practice, from classroom observation\ and from small-scale action
research:

- You need to provide some flexibility in the
  ways in which assignments are presented to
  the class so that although there is one main
  writing task to be completed by all pupils,
  there are also additional optional (or
  extension) tasks. In this way pupils can
  work at different speeds and on different
  assignments within a common context.

- Pupils need to accept the 'ground rules'
  which underpin the flexible organisation of
  work in the classroom so that they settle
  quickly into routines of behaviour and do not
  require constant guidance by the teacher.
  Equally, when working with an individual or
  group, the teacher must be able to continue
  to monitor the behaviour and work of the
  rest of the class.

- If you explain clearly at the outset the
  nature and purpose of the main task you have
  set and what is to count as success in
  completing it, pupils know what is expected
  of them. Most of them can then work with
  greater independence and can attempt to
  monitor their own progress.

- You should try to spread the responsibility
  for formative assessment as widely as possible
  in the classroom so that pupils themselves
  play an increasingly important role in it.

The teacher then ceases to be 'the fount of all knowledge' and the learner begins to accept increasing responsibility for his/her own progress.

- It is unrealistic to aim to provide in-depth help for every pupil every week or even fortnight. It is possible though to adopt a focusing strategy so that the work of a small group of pupils becomes the object of detailed examination for a limited period of time. In this way you can gradually and systematically give formative help to the whole class, building up a thorough knowledge of each individual in the course of a term.

It has been argued in this chapter that the pre-writing phase in the classroom, when a writing task is introduced by the teacher, is of importance to the process of formative assessment in two related ways. First, classroom management is made easier for the teacher if from the outset pupils are set clear goals to work towards; in this way many children will be able to monitor and assess their own progress as they write. Secondly, the feedback offered by the teacher once a draft has been completed can be made more effective if discussion is explicitly related to the aims and purposes of the task and to the exemplification provided in the pre-writing phase.

It is to the pre-writing phase, therefore, that our attention now turns.

Chapter Five

PRE-WRITING ACTIVITIES

The pre-writing phase is an important and often
undervalued part of the total sequence of classroom
activities in the teaching of extended writing. Even
the most able classes may find it difficult to begin
a writing task without some kind of preparation and
guidance, and the nature and extent of the support
that teachers offer to children of 'average
abilities' and to slower-learning pupils is likely
to be even more important. Yet Arthur Applebee
states in his research study of the teaching of
writing across the curriculum that pre-writing
activities in the observed American secondary school
classrooms averaged only just over three minutes -
and 'that included everything from the time the
teacher began introducing the topic until the first
student began to write.' (Applebee 1981 p.74) And
Ernest Spencer in his research study of the teaching
of writing in Scottish secondary schools reports
that many pupils seemed vague about the purposes of
written work. The guidance offered appeared to
consist mainly of brief advice, with the teacher
giving pupils an idea of what they were to do in
the tasks set. 'There was little evidence of any
major effort to develop or explain the skills and
strategies with which pupils could approach the
particular problem of the writing they were about
to do.' (Spencer 1983 pp.33-34)
    There is no simple formula for choosing and
implementing appropriate pre-writing activities, no
correct sequence of events for the teacher to follow.
Teachers favour different teaching styles and organise their classrooms and relate to their pupils in
different ways. Even when they appear to be
exploring similar subjects or themes, they will often
set different kinds of writing task with different
purposes and goals. It is possible, however, to

offer some generalisations and to provide exemplification from classroom work. All the activities to be discussed aim to 'prime' pupils before they put pen to paper on a main writing task and to help them to begin to write with confidence and with a sense of purpose.

In setting a task for extended writing teachers often seek to interest, motivate and stimulate their pupils before they begin to write. A 'stimulus for writing' is frequently used partly with the aim of helping pupils to formulate subject-matter for their writing and partly to create interest and an involvement in the task. This stimulus may take a number of different forms; it can be visual (a picture or television programme, for example), oral/aural (a piece of music, audio-tape or talk by a visiting speaker), experiential (a visit out of school or a role-playing exercise), or, most commonly, in written form (a short story or extract from a novel, a newspaper article or discursive text). A further accepted feature of classroom stimulation would be the teacher's own enthusiasm and his/her ability to communicate to the class a sense of interest in and commitment to a worthwhile task.

When the task itself is set, considerable latitude and freedom are often given to pupils as regards the way they can interpret and tackle the subject. Frequently a choice of different topics is offered and only a limited amount of guidance is given about what will constitute success in completing the task. Children are encouraged to express in writing what they themselves wish to communicate. They can choose a subject they want to write about and decide for themselves how they are going to develop and shape their texts. It is an open, 'child-centred' approach to classroom work. When teachers come to evaluate the work their pupils have produced they adopt the 'flotation' approach to assessment described in the previous chapter. They respond to what their pupils have written, using their own internalised 'plans' for different kinds of writing task, the established classroom rules for writing which they assume all pupils will know and accept, and their knowledge of the achievements (and possibly the behaviour and attitudes) of the individual child whose script is being read and evaluated.

It will be argued in the rest of this chapter that teachers may be able to provide more effective help for their pupils if they attempt to define and elaborate the task to be undertaken more clearly and explicitly at the pre-writing stage, even though this approach may at first be perceived by some readers as being over-directive and didactic.

THE LEVEL OF DIFFICULTY

First, it is possible for teachers to clarify (for their own benefit as well as in the interest of their pupils) the level of difficulty of the task that is to be set. This in turn is likely to influence the teacher's expectations of success and the kinds of assessment criteria that will eventually be selected. When classes have been organised in streams or sets according to the perceived abilities and achievements of the pupils, the problem should be less acute than in a 'mixed ability' class where the range of abilities and achievements in writing are wide. As a result of classroom research which has involved the observation of teachers at work with their pupils, it is now well documented that with mixed ability groups many teachers still tend to pitch the level of difficulty of a lesson at a dominant 'steering group' within the class, usually the pupils of perceived 'average ability'. As a result both the most and least able children tend to be neglected. (Sands and Kerry 1982 Chapters Four and Seven)

Conversely many experienced teachers who work predominantly with slower-learning pupils accept that it is especially important to provide these children with a sense of achievement and success when they complete an assignment. The achievement of success clearly will depend on pupils being set tasks that are within their existing competence and on them being provided with appropriate help and support. Then, when some measure of success has been achieved and recognised, the positive experience it provides will act as an important source of continuing motivation for further classroom work. For example, one teacher commented in interview as follows:

> *(Slower learning pupils) have been in mixed ability classes where they have seen the best and they know how far away they are from it... a lot of them hate writing ... they're so desperate to get it finished that they don't want to think about what they're writing down ... They have a very low opinion of themselves ... and have a low opinion of their work and probably want to forget it ever existed by the time they've finished it ...*

(Roger 1982a)

It is helpful, then, if teachers take account of the
'level of difficulty' when they set an assignment
involving extended writing, both in terms of the
intrinsic difficulty of the task itself and in terms
of the nature and degree of help offered by the
teacher. Some writing tasks are likely to be
inherently more difficult than others. And, to
write at length with little or no preparation or
support (as in many tests of writing) is the most
demanding kind of context for writing of all.

Discussion of the writing process in Chapters
Two and Three helps to clarify the notion of a
gradient of difficulty that is intrinsic to different
kinds of writing task likely to be set by teachers.
This gradient of difficulty will depend on the
potential cognitive and linguistic demands placed on
the writer and upon the task's context and purpose,
rather than on the writer's own response to the task.
An experienced writer can, after all, readily
transform an apparently simple topic into a complex,
demanding text, or equally may be able to simplify a
task that on the surface appears difficult and
complicated. In other words, when teachers set classroom writing tasks, there is likely to be a potential
'continuum of difficulty' from the easiest to the
most difficult level according to:

- whether or not the subject-matter of the
  writing involves the thoughts, vocabulary and
  language structures which are close to the
  writer's everyday life and communicative
  experience as opposed to the more contrived
  and deliberately organised structures of
  'transactional' or 'poetic' writing

- whether or not the perceived audience for the
  writing is familiar and limited in number, as
  opposed to an audience that is large, impersonal and unknown

- whether or not the tone of the piece is
  informal as opposed to formal

- whether or not the subject-matter is concrete
  as opposed to abstract

By using this framework, it is possible to produce
two models or stereotypes of writing tasks that are
likely to be intrinsically the easiest and the most
difficult for children. An 'easy' task would require
writers to organise and articulate subject-matter

that is close to their lives and immediate interests
and to deal with it in a concrete way; it would be
directed towards a known reader (like the teacher or
peer group) and be informal in style and tone. On
the other hand, a 'difficult' task would deal with
abstract subject-matter outside the immediate experience and interests of the writer and it would be
cognitively demanding; it would be directed towards
an unknown, impersonal reader and be formal in style
and tone.

These two contrasting models of writing
difficulty can be illustrated by short extracts from
different pieces of writing by two secondary pupils
of average ability and attainment. The first is a
personal, expressive account of the trauma of getting
up on a cold morning; it is written by a pupil in her
first term at secondary school:

> *GETTING UP ON A COLD MORNING*
> *The first thing that came into focus was my*
> *curtains and window. I hate my curtains.*
> *They're a horrible brown colour with red and*
> *yellow blotches on and black lines joining them*
> *up. I grunted and turned over again. My door*
> *was slightly ajar and suddenly a small black*
> *shape came dashing in and next thing I knew it*
> *had jumped on my bed, landed full in my middle,*
> *and stuffed its foot down my ear. 'Get your*
> *foot out me ear,' I mumbled. It was Henry my*
> *black kitten. She made her way up to the top*
> *of my bed sticking her other paw into my eyes*
> *hoping to get some sleep, but Henry decided*
> *she'd had enough, so she stood up and ran to the*
> *top of my bed and back out of the door. 'Yeow,'*
> *I yelled, 'Stop scratching'. Once more I shut*
> *my eyes and snuggled down into my bed again.*
> *Thump, thump, thump came to my ears. 'Oh no,'*
> *I thought, 'Tommy's coming to tell me to get*
> *up.' 'Ann, Ann' he yelled, 'It's time to get*
> *up.' 'And don't I know it,' I mumbled. I got*
> *slowly out of bed and crept to the window and*
> *drew the curtains. All I saw was a world white*
> *with snow. 'Cor,' I thought, 'Perhaps we won't*
> *have to go to school...'*

Ann

It is a lively, engaging piece of writing with a
'ring of truth' about it and an easy, flowing con-
versational style. The task itself, though, was not
a difficult one. The class was asked to write a
personal narrative about a subject close to their

everyday experience. An informal style was appropriate and they were writing for a clearly defined audience (teacher and peers) who could readily understand and share their feelings.

By way of contrast, in this second example an older writer (Tina, aged 15) is struggling with the task of organising and communicating in writing arguments about the nature of violence in society:

> *MY VIEWS ON VIOLENCE*
> *Violence is horrible.*
>
> *Guns and knives people being killed and injured. I think violence is silly and childish, killing other people just because they do not believe in the same things as you.*
>
> *Wreaking places just for fun. Hurting animals and people. Breaking windows in houses, wreaking homes for people who have not done anything wrong.*
>
> *I think the whole thing is downright stupid and those who make trouble should have the same done back to them which they would not like.*
>
> Tina

In this case, although the subject that has been set is also in a sense closely related to pupils' knowledge and understanding, the class was not asked to produce a narrative to describe a single violent incident. The topic is more abstract: it requires them to argue a case and to try to persuade the reader that their views are valid. The audience for the writing on this occasion is more impersonal and remote and the style required is more formal. It is a potentially much more difficult task than the first example and Tina obviously needed more help and advice in tackling it. Although she communicates a sense of concern and sincerity in her writing, the structures she uses are closer to what is appropriate to an oral context than to written forms. She offers a series of abrupt assertions with meanings implied rather than communicated explicitly. And although her writing may have some of the compactness and intensity of free verse, it lacks the coherence of discursive prose.

DEFINING THE NATURE AND PURPOSE OF THE TASK

Explanation by the teacher for the benefit of the whole class is obviously helpful if it clarifies the nature and purpose of the task pupils will have to complete and if the task in question can be related to the whole context of classroom work they are engaged in. Children are likely to value a writing task more highly if they can see its point and purpose and if they can be helped to form a clear sense of audience for it. Such pre-writing instructions can be conveyed to the class both orally and in writing and can be elaborated and reinforced by the teacher's and by pupils' own questions and by the use of blackboard or overhead projector to summarise or illustrate aspects of the assignment.

For example, in the first of two recorded classroom extracts that follow, the teacher seeks to explain to a group of slower-learning pupils in a secondary school how they are to set about writing a simulated newspaper report on a topic of current interest. This particular lesson forms part of a series in the course of which pupils have examined and discussed the contents of a daily newspaper and have been introduced to the key organising questions that will have to be answered in their written reports (the 'six honest serving men' which the teacher refers to in the extract):

Teacher   *What I'd like you to do today is take a sideways step. You see where it says at the top* (of the worksheet) *to take an article from your paper? What I'd like you to do is ... well, if you've started that, fair enough, but if you haven't then leave it, because what I'd like you to do at this stage is to make up your own newspaper article. Now if you're going to do that, what must you do? What must you have in it?*

Pupil 1   *News.*

Teacher   *And how am I going to know it's news? What key things have I got to have?*

Pupil 2   *Contents.*

Teacher   *What's the contents going to be?*

Pupil 1   *What page you'll find it on.*

Teacher   *No ... no ... You're going to make up one of your own. You're going to write a news article, say, you could write about the day of action or whatever ... the bodies that were found in Beirut ...*

	The Prime Minister's visit to Japan or something like that.
Pupil 1	*(inaudible)*
Teacher	*So you're going to write your own newspaper article. So how are you going to do it? What things must you have in it?*
Pupil 3	*A headline*
Teacher	*Sometimes. You don't always have a headline. If you look at your ...* (paper) *sometimes they don't have a big headline. Sometimes they have things like ... in the 'World News' Section - sometimes it doesn't have a headline, it just has a little note like that. We were talking about the content. Somebody mentioned content ... what must I have in it?*
Pupil 2	*Stories.*
Teacher	*So how am I going to set about the story? How am I going to build up the story? What important things must I have for the story to make sense? Stephen?*
Pupil 1	*Words?*
Teacher	*Right. You've got to have words. You're sitting looking at something very important that you spent ages copying out* (a worksheet)
Pupil 1	*A draft.*
Teacher	*No, that's not a draft. What does that say?*
Pupil 1	*News stories.*
Teacher	*No, what does the thing underneath it say?*
Pupil 1	*'I have six honest serving men.'*
Teacher	*Right, read it off.*
Pupil 1	*'They taught me all I knew. Their names are what and why and when and how and where and who.'*
Teacher	*O.K. What d'you think we're going to have to do in this story?*
Pupil 1	*Put, well, what's happening.*
Pupil 2	*Why?*
Teacher	*Why it happened, if possible why it happened.*
Pupil 4	*How did it happen?*
Teacher	*Right, it's as simple as that. So any story you write you've got to have these bits of information in it ...*

There is obviously some unanticipated confusion for the teacher in the course of her questioning at the beginning of the extract because of the misinterpretation of the term 'Contents' which Pupil 1 takes to mean the contents page of a book. The same pupil also wrongly anticipates that the teacher is leading up to the writing of the first draft of their reports. However, the teacher's main planning point about the 'six honest serving men' is eventually successfully made and she goes on to reinforce and develop it.

In the second extract a teacher in a different school (but in a similar context) explains to the whole class the importance of using a sketch map to help clarify a written report. The class in question is a low-achieving third-year group in a secondary school and the task that they are about to begin is the main assignment in a unit of work which explores the theme 'Witnesses'. The assignment involves a written report of a fictitious robbery from a high street bank which they have 'observed' from different points of view; an audio-tape has also been used by the teacher to present a simulated news broadcast of the event.

> *I mentioned to you yesterday but this is the detail of it; this is how it works.* (The following is illustrated throughout on the blackboard). *I'll give you two examples of what I'm talking about. It's the plan. I think for a lot of you this is straightforward, so let me do it quickly, so that I don't waste anybody's time.*
>
> *The original bank-raid on the tape took place in a bank on the corner of a street and the door was <u>there</u> like that, and presumably the van was parked outside. If you were writing about that one, you would have to decide, as I said yesterday, where the witness was. Now let's say the witness was in fact walking up the road and round the corner to the bus stop which is <u>here</u>.*
>
> *There must have been some point at which he first saw people either going in or coming out of the bank. If he continued to walk, there must have been a point at which he lost sight of them because the van would be in the way. That is difficult to think up in your head. If you put it down on the map it becomes obvious...*

(Roger 1982b)

In the first extract the teacher was working informally with a group of pupils who were sitting at their desks. She was trying to tease out important planning points by means of the questions she asked. In this second extract the teacher is working more formally with the whole class, trying to show them how a diagram can help to clarify the content of a written report. Although explaining and questioning are part of a teacher's traditional classroom skills and are usually associated with expository whole class teaching, the skills can clearly be successfully applied to work either with groups or with an individual pupil.

As an alternative to these strategies (or in addition to them) the teacher's instructions about the nature and goals of a writing task can be conveyed to a class in written form. Figure 5.1 for example, shows the second teacher's pre-writing checklist for a task in a different unit of work. The checklist seeks to give clear guidelines to the same group of pupils who are about to begin writing a narrative on the theme 'Boy Meets Girl'. In the checklist reference is made to a schools' television film ('Ties': *Scene* BBC TV) which the class had seen and discussed in preparation for the writing of their own story.

CRITERIA FOR SUCCESS

The kind of written checklist that is illustrated in Figure 5.1 can be developed further in order to provide pupils with a fuller statement about which features of their writing will be important when the teacher comes to assess a written draft or evaluate the final script. The checklist can help to give pupils an increased sense of purpose and direction when they begin to write and the teacher's provision of clear objectives at an early stage does not necessarily act as a constraint; it can free pupils to work with greater independence and confidence while they are actually engaged on the task. However, if you do attempt to produce a valid pre-writing checklist and to provide pupils with your anticipated criteria for judging eventual success, initially you are likely to be faced by (at least) three identifiable problems. The first is a problem of self-awareness; the second is the problem of which criteria out of possibly many to select; and the third, the problem of how to communicate to your pupils the selection you do eventually decide on.

As regards the problem of self-awareness, it is not always easy for us to make clear and explicit to ourselves what is going to count as success when our pupils eventually complete the writing tasks we

CHECKLIST FOR MAIN WRITING TASK

```
Boy Meets Girl

Writing Assignment 1.

Write the story of an outing where a girl/boy
meets a boy/girl.  At first she/he doesn't
like him/her but in the course of the story
they gradually change their attitude and
come to like each other.  (If you like you
could use the characters and the setting of
'Ties' for your story).

It is important that

1   your story involve a limited number of
    characters and that the main characters
    should be described well

2   the outing is fully described          and

3   the story should be long enough and detailed
    enough for you to show the gradual changes
    which take place in the attitudes of the
    main characters

Before you start writing the first draft of
your story make notes in answer to the
following questions

a)   The Outing  What kind of outing is it?
                 When does it take place?
                 Where do the characters go?
                 Why do they go on the outing?

b)   The Boy     Who is he?
                 What is his name?
                 How old is he?
                 What is he like?
     (You may find it helpful to refer to the
      list of words for describing people
      which you already have)

c)   The Girl    Who is she?
                 What is her name?
                 How old is she?
                 What is she like?
```

Figure 5.1: Checklist for Writing Task - 'Boy Meets
           Girl' (Peacock and Roger 1984 p.147)

set; it is much easier and more convenient simply to wait and see what they write and then to respond appropriately. We can then be influenced by the way the task has been interpreted and by our knowledge of the pupil who has completed it. In fact, we can use the 'flotation' approach to assessment that has already been described and discussed in the previous chapter. Alternatively, a useful starting point in seeking to solve this first fundamental problem is to try to analyse the nature of the task you are about to set. In more practical terms you have to ask yourself the question, 'What will my pupils have to *do* in order to complete the task successfully?' To be able to answer this question you will probably first need to become more aware of the detailed cognitive 'plans' for writing you already possess. Then you will have to try to make explicit to yourself the qualities that are likely to be essential for success in completing this particular task, and finally try to make these qualities clear to your pupils before they begin work.

At first this is not an easy exercise. In my experience teachers rarely provide an exhaustive initial list. When at the formative assessment stage, they begin to match their anticipated criteria against the scripts the pupils have actually produced, almost always they find they have overlooked something of importance that they had taken for granted at the planning stage. Sometimes, too, they find a clear mismatch between the criteria they initially anticipated and those they found themselves actually applying in assessing a particular piece of work. An extreme example of this would be the case of a teacher who claimed at the planning stage that she would be looking for a range of ambitious qualities when she responded to pupils' work, but when she analysed tape-recordings of her discussions with pupils and the comments she wrote on their scripts, she discovered that in fact she tended to concentrate on the surface features of spelling, punctuation and capital letters.

It is tempting and relatively easy to create unrealistic criteria for success at the beginning of a phase of work as a remote, theoretical exercise and to apply quite different criteria in the reality of the classroom when working under pressure. We all have aspirations about what we want to achieve as teachers. It is often a salutary experience for us to examine what in contrast we seem to stress in the classroom and what we are sometimes prepared to settle for. It is worth reflecting too on the

nature of our pupils' perceptions of their achievements, as relayed to them by the behaviour of their
teachers.

However, as confidence and awareness grow, it
becomes increasingly possible to create long and
detailed checklists which tabulate all the qualities
you may anticipate in setting a writing task.
Clearly it is important to be realistic about the
demands you are making on your pupils and about how
much can be achieved in the normal classroom context.
Pupils should not be overwhelmed with too much
detail; you need to decide what is most important
in the completion of a particular task and to concentrate pupils' attention on selected criteria. There
is no single correct way to make this selection.
Although different teachers may set apparently
similar tasks, their purposes and objectives may be
in some way different, and clearly different kinds of
writing task will require different emphases in the
selection of criteria. For example, in assignments
which involve personal, imaginative writing,
accuracy of spelling and appropriate punctuation will
not necessarily be important criteria for some
teachers, whereas these same features would be of
considerable importance in the writing of a formal
business letter. Selected criteria can be communicated to pupils both orally and in writing. A
written checklist which is glossed and reinforced
orally by the teacher in the classroom can continue
to act as a support and source of guidance to pupils
while they are working on their drafts and can be a
helpful starting point for comment in formative
discussion once the draft has been completed. A
proposed framework for such a checklist (Peacock and
Roger 1984 p.158) uses the following headings:

> *SUBJECT (or Content)*
> *POINT OF VIEW*
> *REGISTER*
> *ORGANISATION*
> *MECHANICS (or Graphological Conventions)*

In this case the heading *Mechanics* is deliberately
placed last in the list so that surface features
like spelling, punctuation and handwriting do not
become the main focus of the teacher's or the
pupil's attention. It is also important to emphasise two further points about the use of this and
similar checklists which teachers may themselves
compose. First, the kind of success that is being
looked for on a task does not necessarily have to be

absolute. It is not essential, for example, to insist on complete accuracy in spelling. Secondly, although abstract headings like 'Register' may well require glossing at first, pupils do not appear to experience serious difficulties in comprehending or using them.

USING A MODEL OF SUCCESS

Task analysis is one appropriate strategy for teachers to use when they select criteria for success at the pre-writing stage. An alternative and at first perhaps a more accessible strategy is the analysis by the teacher of a written model which has been chosen to exemplify success. A piece of writing is selected by the teacher because it demonstrates success to pupils in a concrete and attainable form. There is no reason why you should choose for this purpose an ideal that children can only aspire to but never hope to attain. It has to be a piece of writing that they can relate to and which they can hope to match. Consequently texts written by non-professional authors or by inexperienced writers, like the pupils themselves, are usually more suitable for this purpose than works of outstanding literary merit or texts by professional authors.

The teacher can examine and reflect on an exemplar of this kind and judge the qualities it exhibits. The appropriate features of the model you select can be incorporated into your classroom preparation for a main writing task. It can be used to elaborate and illustrate aspects of the assignment in the course of classroom explanation and discussion. And it can continue to act as a source of support to pupils when they begin to write. They can refer to the model when they review their drafts and it can be used as a source of illustration and comparison in the course of formative discussion.

When used in this way the model of success can act as a concrete example of what can be achieved by writers not unlike the pupils themselves. It is intended to provide illustration and support; it is *not* a text to be simply copied or imitated in laborious detail. A model that has been read and discussed at the pre-writing stage is likely to influence the way the majority of pupils interpret and set about a writing assignment. But its use by the teacher does not of necessity entail a convergent approach to a task with all pupils in a class eventually creating a similar or even an identical text. In fact divergence and an individual inter-

pretation of a task could be included in the
teacher's explicit criteria for success. Whatever
the subject set, all pupils are free to select their
own words and organise them in such a way as to
communicate a unique set of meanings.

In practice, when a traditional stimulus for
writing is presented to a class at the pre-writing
stage, it often becomes an implicit model for
children's own writing. If a story like 'Let's
Play Poison', for example, is read and discussed by
the teacher and class before pupils begin to write,
features of the plot, narrative and characterisation
will tend to re-appear in recognisable forms in
pupils' scripts, even though in other respects (as
with Kevin's piece, discussed in the previous
chapter) the subject-matter and treatment are
individual and distinctive. The recorded television
programme 'Ties' was also used as a deliberate model
when pupils completed the task on the theme 'Boy
Meets Girl'. Explicit references were made to
aspects of the programme by the teacher in the pre-
writing phases of explanation and discussion when
the task was introduced and in the checklist he
provided (see Figure 5.1).

The film 'Ties' gives an account of what
happens when two sisters impulsively decide to drive
to a seaside town in the summer and shows their
different and changing responses to the boys they
meet there. Watching and discussing the film undoubtedly influenced the ways in which most pupils
developed the narrative of their own stories and
presented the characters who took part. However,
unlike a written model, the videotape was not available for individual reference when the class was
engaged on the task and the narrative demonstrated
by the programme was essentially visual in nature.
Unlike the writing task the class was attempting to
complete, the meanings of the television film were
communicated to the audience principally by visual
means, with supporting dialogue, not by means of
language alone.

PLANNING

The preparation of some kind of plan to help pupils
tackle a writing assignment is a well established
activity in the pre-writing phase of classroom work.
Most typically teachers seem to work formally with
the whole class; they use the blackboard or overhead
projector to summarise and organise suggestions for
the writing assignment, emphasising and elaborating

ideas which are accepted from the pupils. Alternatively, they may work more informally with a small
group, directing discussion towards a particular
individual's work. For example, an experienced
teacher makes the following comments in interview:

> *I would suggest they do a plan of what they're*
> *going to do. I'd say 'Tell me how your story*
> *begins', and I would probably sit down and*
> *plan it with them, and then give them this*
> *paragraph and say, 'Now you write your story*
> *and in paragraph one put all of this ...'*
> *and show them how to organise it properly.*
>
> (Roger 1982a)

Another strategy that seems to be frequently adopted
is to ask the class or individuals to volunteer
suggestions for key words that are suitable to the
subject set and for the resulting list to be collat-
ed and displayed. (Alternatively the teacher can
simply provide a list of appropriate words). In
both cases the aim is to create some kind of
structure for a writing task and to give pupils
'the confidence to use lots of words which they
haven't used before in many cases not words that
they don't know but words which often they haven't
the confidence to put down' *(Ibid)*. One problem
associated with the 'key words' approach is that the
strategy often acts as a constraint that shapes
the writer's response to a task. If you are trying
to communicate a unique message in writing, it is
your own words that you need to select and organise,
not someone else's. For this reason it is always
difficult to suggest vocabulary for other writers
either at the planning stage or while they are
actually engaged on an extended 'own words' assignment. It is often only when you have read a
completed draft that you begin to understand what
it is a writer is trying to communicate.

Whole class discussion seems to be always led
(and often dominated) by the teacher when a suitable
plan for an assignment is established and elaborated.
After discussion of this kind pupils go on to
develop their own plans, trying to anticipate and
organise the development of the drafts they will
eventually produce. For example, one pupil drew up
the following outline in preparation for her 'Boy
Meets Girl' narrative, using the checklist provided
by the teacher (Figure 5.1) to help her to sketch
out her plan:

> *(a) Outing to Blackpool in summer*
> *(b) Julie is on holiday*
> *She is quiet*
> *(c) She likes to go to discos*
> *She meets Eric*
> *Eric comes from Birmingham*
> *(d) Eric approaches Julie*
> *Said some stupid things*
> *Julie dislikes Eric*
> *The disco is in the town*
> *Say how they begin to like each other*
> *Make them friends*
> *Then end with a happy ending.*
>
> (Roger 1982b)

A writer's plan does not have to be set out in this way, as a chronological sequence, although it is a conventional approach. It could in this case be organised as a 'map'. The outing to Blackpool would be the central focus for the plan with other aspects of the story connected to it by 'spokes' and arranged around it in random order (See Figure 5.2). This form of outline - a 'mind map' or 'spider plan' - has a number of advantages over the more conventional kind of plan organised in a linear sequence. It is potentially more open and less structured, and the main ideas can be arranged on the paper in any order. They have to be organised and put in an appropriate order only when the writer begins to work on the first draft. Also, as in the case of the model and checklist, the 'map' (like a conventional plan) remains as a source of reference during the course of writing and reviewing and can be used by the teacher to help give a focus to formative discussion with the writer.

THE ROLE OF DISCUSSION

Classroom discussion is now widely accepted as an essential feature of pre-writing preparation. Purposeful talk in the classroom can be valuable in its own right, of course, and pupils can gain in oral fluency, social skills and confidence as a result of being involved in different kinds of oral tasks that prepare the way for their first written drafts. However, discussion can also act as an important form of planning, preparation and rehearsal for a main writing task. It can help pupils to begin to formulate and articulate their thoughts before they begin to communicate them in written form. New ideas can be sparked off as they listen

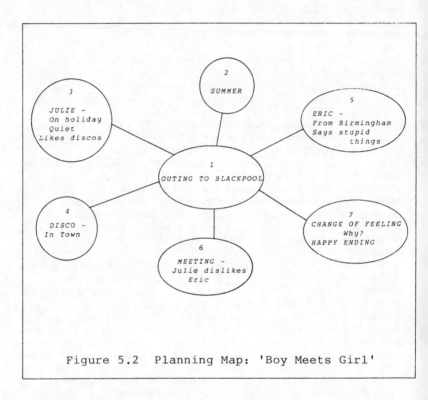

Figure 5.2   Planning Map: 'Boy Meets Girl'

to others talking and pupils may be helped to recall subject-matter that will be relevant to the task that is to be attempted. Talking and listening, then, can be important sources of 'priming' before writing helping pupils to rehearse what they will eventually include in their written drafts.

The teacher can organise discussion either as a whole class event or in small groups or pairs. Although it is a commonly adopted strategy, whole class discussion can again easily be dominated by the teacher and sometimes hardly counts as discussion at all. The teacher tends to talk for a large proportion of the time that is available and only a limited number of pupils are able to add comments or ask questions. It is often difficult for every child to be heard in this context and those who are shy and lack confidence find it difficult to participate in a large, public audience.

In contrast, in group discussion pupils are more independent; they can express themselves at greater length in a more reassuring, less inhibiting context. On the other hand, discussion in groups can be more demanding for the teacher in terms of planning and management in the classroom. Some kind of worksheet is normally needed to give discussion a clear sense of purpose and direction, and groups tend to be noisier and can be more difficult to control than a more tightly directed class. In managing group work, teachers have to move constantly from group to group in order to listen to discussion and, if appropriate, to contribute to it, but at the same time they have to be able to monitor the behaviour of the whole class and their apparent progress being made on the task. Obviously this mode of learning is more likely to succeed and management problems will be less acute if pupils understand and accept from the beginning the ground rules that apply in such contexts so that classroom routines run smoothly.

Classroom discussion played an important part in the pre-writing preparation of all the main tasks that have been described and discussed in this chapter. The writing of the simulated newspaper report, for example, was preceded by the examination and discussion in groups of copies of national newspapers. The teacher provided worksheets to give direction to the pupils' investigation and the search and discussion were organised under a variety of headings. The teacher tended to address the whole class only at the start and conclusion of lessons and at key comments within lessons to convey information or instructions.

In preparation for the 'Boy Meets Girl' narrative, the teacher provided advertising material from a computer-dating firm which he discussed initially with the whole class. The class then worked in pairs filling in a simulated computer-dating questionnaire and discussing the appropriate characteristics to look for in a partner. The showing (and re-showing) of the videotape of the schools' broadcast 'Ties' also promoted considerable whole-class and paired discussion. The move from whole-class explanation and teacher-led discussion to clearly defined tasks (with supporting worksheets) and discussion in pairs was a characteristic of this second teacher's professional methodology.

The relationship between exploratory talk in the classroom and children's increased understanding has been much researched and widely discussed in

recent years; it is not appropriate to attempt to
provide a further detailed exploration of the subject
here. However, in conclusion, it is worth comment-
ing that in the course of the preparatory pre-
writing activities that have been described and discussed in this chapter pupils were engaged in varied
work in all four language modes. They produced
written notes and plans, for example; they talked and
listened to the teacher and each other; they watched
and listened to varied audio-visual materials; they
read and responded to worksheets, checklists and
longer written texts. For most pupils the eventual
activity of creating a first written draft was
therefore embedded in and dependent upon an extended
and unified language context which prepared the way
for the main writing task and involved all four
language modes.

We have dwelt on the pre-writing phase at some
length in this chapter in order to reinforce a growing acceptance among teachers concerning the
importance of 'priming' pupils before they begin
work on an extended writing task. In addition,
though, we have argued that pre-writing activities
in the classroom should be explicitly linked to the
process of formative assessment after pupils have
completed their first drafts. In this way children
can be given clearer guidance about the aims of the
assignment that has been set and the level of success
they achieve in completing it. When this connection
has been effectively established, the problem of
helping pupils to develop and improve as writers can
be tackled more systematically and with greater
confidence.

This key problem of how teachers can help
pupils to improve as writers forms the subject-
matter of our next chapter.

Chapter Six

HELPING CHILDREN TO IMPROVE AS WRITERS

The process of formative assessment will involve
more than simply identifying strengths and weaknesses
in a writer's script. It is not only diagnostic in
nature; some form of action is anticipated. The
teacher who reads a child's draft needs to be able
to help the pupil to overcome perceived difficulties
and to develop and improve as a writer. To be able
to assist in this way we have argued that a teacher
needs to understand the nature of the demands made
by the writing process itself in all its complexities and also to possess professional skills that
will enable children to learn effectively. One
essential aspect of these professional skills is a
repertoire of classroom strategies which help
children to understand better the nature of their
difficulties in writing and which help them to work
at these problems with a sense of purpose and some
satisfaction of eventual success.
    When they work on a shared writing task, child-
ren are likely to experience a variety of difficulties and they will almost certainly learn to overcome
their individual problems in different ways. When
teachers work under pressure in the classroom with
constant demands being made on their time and attention, they inevitably find it difficult to give
adequate attention to a single child in order to
diagnose individual difficulties and to select the
most appropriate approach for an individual learning
style. Despite this pressure, teaching strategies
should not be thought of as convenient, pre-packaged
solutions to children's writing problems; they must
be seen as one part only of the total classroom
context. To be successful, different kinds of
strategy need to take account of the purposes and
goals of an assignment and the pre-writing support
that was provided. Above all teachers need to value

the importance of the 'climate for learning' and the
rules and routines that they often intuitively
establish in the classroom. Without this supportive
classroom context, no learning strategy is likely to
succeed, no matter how innovative or potentially
illuminating it may be.

The purpose of this chapter, then, is to direct
attention in particular to that phase of classroom
work which involves the revision of a script and the
attempt to produce an improved draft, when the
teacher seeks to help a single individual, a group
of pupils or even a whole class, or when pupils try
to help themselves or each other. Some of the
strategies that are to be described and discussed
are well known and long established, but it is hoped
that they will be seen in a new light; others are
more recent and innovative. What is offered is a
critical overview of different kinds of approach
rather than a definitive or exhaustive account of the
possibilities open to a teacher. For more comprehensive and detailed accounts the reader is directed to
other texts (Haley-James 1981, Scardamalia *et al*
1981, and Shaughnessy 1977, for example).

DRAFTING AND REDRAFTING

An essential feature of the formative assessment of
writing is the opportunity given to pupils to draft
and redraft their work. After a writing task has
been introduced by the teacher and different kinds
of pre-writing support provided, pupils make their
first attempts at drafting a response to the topic.
When these drafts have been completed to the pupils'
own satisfaction, the teacher (or other pupils)
intervene both to encourage and reinforce successful
features of each script and to provide advice and
help so that the draft can be improved. If necessary
a number of drafts can be made by the writer; scripts
can be continually revised and improved until they
meet the criteria for success that were initially
set by the teacher or by the writers themselves or
until an acceptable standard is reached.

The drafting and redrafting sequence can be
illustrated by the work of one primary school pupil,
nine-year old Adele. The main writing task to be
discussed was set within a unit of classroom work
which explored the lives of people working in
travelling shops in an imaginary local community.
Along with the rest of her class, Adele produced a
narrative on the theme of a 'personal disaster'
which had been experienced in the course of a day's

work. Pre-writing support for the assignment
included the teacher discussing with the whole class
the purpose and audience for the story and explaining
how this task related to the work already completed.
The children also discussed in groups what they were
intending to write about and they drew outlines in
picture form to show clearly the sequence of events
involved. A word-bank which had been compiled in
the course of the project from the teacher's and
children's suggestions was also available.

Adele's story takes the form of two preparatory
drafts followed by the final account for publication
to the class. After each of the first two drafts
the teacher intervened to help Adele improve and
develop what she had written. As can be seen, the
three versions are quite distinct as regards content
and language; the final account is in addition more
carefully and neatly presented than the first two
preparatory drafts. The three different versions of
her text are accompanied by the teacher's own
commentary about the development of Adele's story,
the parts played by both teacher and pupil in improving it, and how the final outcome was achieved:

FIRST DRAFT

*One day I went a little walk by my self wene I
came back my engine was on fire I Phone the
fire brigad they put water on it my van was all
burnt I was very sade but I got a new van for
nuthing I was very happy and I wasnt sade eny
more.*

'During discussion with Adele about her first
draft there were three points I wanted to make.
The first was her assumption that the reader
knows who she is and that she has a van. The
second point was also about detail. In her
drawings and in earlier discussion Adele had
described the fire well, but there is no description of it in her story at all. We also
talked about the need to explain why she was
alone in the van and where she was when the fire
started. The third point related to the spelling of the word "sad". I wanted to find out
whether her mis-spelling was simply a careless
mistake or indicated a problem. So I decided
to wait until she produced a second draft.
Adele herself pointed out that she had forgotten
to put in full stops apart from one at the end.'

SECOND DRAFT (reproduced at Figure 6.1)

One day it was my tea brak it was a lovly day
and I was very hot, I was by my self.   I left
the van in the cash incary in the car park.
wen I came out my engine was on fure.   I
phoned the fire brigad.   thay came in ther van
they got the fire hose out.   my van was all
burnt and I had to pay 200 punds for another van.
I was very sade.

'Adele's second draft shows how she has tried
to give greater detail to improve the content
of her story. She has also used full-stops
to indicate sentence boundaries but is less
successful with the use of capital letters.
She has changed the ending to explain why she
felt sad, but she still hasn't included a
description of the burning van, so we worked on
the vocabulary she would need to describe the
fire. I circled spelling errors in her second
draft and wrote the correct form below for
Adele to use. As the mis-spelling of "sad"
recurred, I gave the word particular attention
and discovered that she was also adding a final
 e to similar words like "mad" and "bad". We
revised the correct spelling of these words,
therefore, and ensured Adele knew how to spell
them.'

FINAL VERSION

It was my tea break.   It was a lovly day.   So I
went to sit on the grass.   And I had my tea
break there.   My other friends were with me
too.   After my tea break I went to the cash and
carry.   I got all the food and frut.   When I
came out my van was on fire.   I phoned the fire
brigade.   they came.   The got the fire hose
out and put water on the fire, all the smoke
and sparks and flames.   all of my van was all
burnt.   I had to pay 200 pounds four another
one.   I was very sad.

'All together, I was pleased with the work Adele
produced and so was Adele. The children are
aware that their first draft is only the beginning of the process whereby they create an
acceptable piece of writing and it will not be
used to emphasise their failure. Adele is only
beginning to write continuously and my assess-

ment therefore was based more on content and effectiveness than on the correctness of her work ...'

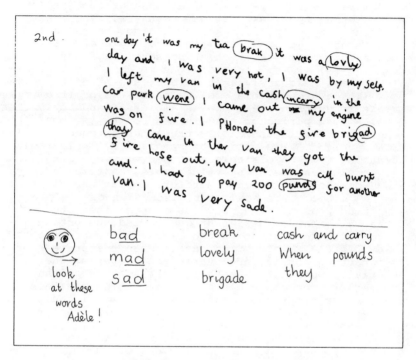

Figure 6.1   Adele's Second Draft

Adele's work has clearly developed and improved in the course of redrafting; the subject-matter of the second and final draft becomes more detailed and interesting and important changes are made in each version in addition to the revisions to spelling and punctuation included in the final account.   In fact some of the changes where detail is added (in the final draft, for example, when the fire brigade arrives) upset the flow of the style, making expression appear awkward.

A teacher clearly needs to be able to provide different kinds of help when a pupil is trying to develop and improve a draft, but it is important at this initial stage of our discussion to be realistic about the difficulties that face teachers in the classroom when they seek to implement the redrafting

81

sequence that has been described. To help children to learn effectively, the teacher must allow them adequate time to work at their difficulties and to achieve the satisfaction of a sense of success in completing the task that has been set. The first attempt that a pupil makes should not be the only one that is judged and evaluated. However, it will be readily accepted that at present many less successful writers seem anxious to complete a classroom task as quickly as possible (and often to write as little as possible too). Teachers find it difficult to sustain their pupils' interest and motivation for a long period of time in many contexts, but perhaps this is especially true when extended writing is involved. The notion of spending a considerable span of time on a single extended writing task (with an assignment using up valuable lesson time for days and perhaps weeks) may therefore appear unrealistic.

On the other hand, our discussion of the prewriting phase in the previous chapter indicated that a number of different and varied supporting activities can go on in the classroom to prepare the way for the main writing task. When the process of redrafting begins, such variety of interest and activity need not be totally lost. It is neither necessary nor desirable for pupils to concentrate all their efforts on the activity of writing alone, as exemplification from the rest of this chapter will show.

The introduction of the writing task in the preparatory phase, the involvement of the pupils in it, and their acceptance of its value and purpose are important aspects of positive motivation in the classroom. But a further (and often undervalued) feature of the approach that is being advocated is the motivation that is provided by the experience of success as pupils work on the task. It is essential therefore, as Adele's teacher emphasised, that initial success is encouraged in the first response a teacher makes to a submitted script. And it is equally important that pupils are made aware that they are making progress while they continue to work on subsequent drafts. As we have seen, although at present pupils spend a lot of time in classrooms engaged in the actual activity of writing, this activity does not always appear to make a significant contribution to their becoming more successful and effective writers.

Experienced writers recognise that redrafting involves more than simply producing a 'fair copy' of what they have written in a first preparatory draft.

They accept too that they will probably make changes as they actually plan and write. They are prepared to make fundamental alterations to the ways in which their meaning is organised and expressed as well as making minor revisions and corrections to surface features. Recent and varied research into the ways in which writers appear to tackle different tasks shows (apparently paradoxically) that mature and proficient writers seem to produce *less* in the way of actual text in a given period of time than less assured and successful writers. (Humes 1983) This seems to be because an experienced writer spends much more time in planning, reviewing and evaluating the text that is being produced and much less time in making the essential marks on the page. In contrast a beginning or inexperienced writer is much more concerned with getting a basic communication conveyed in written form. Good writers appear to make long pauses for thinking and planning between spurts of rapid transcription, whereas unsuccessful writers seem to pause much more, worrying about the actual mechanical processes of writing.

When they review what they have written, poor writers seem to concentrate on checking for obvious errors (which they often fail to recognise). If they make independent changes to their scripts, they tend to alter a single word or phrase rather than attempt to shape their text more effectively by restructuring it. They need constantly to re-read what they have written in order to keep a sense of direction and coherence while they are engaged in producing a written text.

It should not surprise us, then, if many pupils seem to make only limited progress when they redraft their work, even when they invest considerable effort in it. Much of their energy may go into producing the first draft and they have to be helped to understand what is entailed in revising and re-drafting what they have written. With the first draft complete, they may see the task as fundamentally over, believing that the content has been communicated and only 'corrections' have to be made to it. As teachers of writing, therefore, we should not expect too much of the redrafting process, looking from the outset for fundamental changes in children's work and rapid developments. We may have to help our pupils to make the long, slow and difficult transi-tion towards becoming writers who constantly question, review and develop what they have written. Under-standing the nature of the revising process may therefore be more important to the inexperienced

writer than any changes in a text that actually
appear on the page. And what may be crucial, of
course, to this growth of understanding and awareness is the nature of the help that we as teachers
can provide.

The advent of the word processor in the classroom offers us an important opportunity in this
field. Word processors take much of the drudgery
out of the actual activity of re-drafting, they
make the fundamental revision of a text relatively
easy to accomplish, and they ensure a final printed
product of high quality for all pupils. At present,
though, a word processor acts only as an additional
resource in most schools; it cannot yet be viewed as
a replacement for the accepted medium of paper and
pencil.

SHOWING

Probably the most common approach adopted by
teachers in order to help their pupils to improve
as writers is to demonstrate how they themselves
would tackle a problem. This can be done by changing aspects of a draft either in the presence or
absence of the pupil (using the conference or
'postal' methods of formative assessment discussed
in Chapter Four). By demonstrating how a text can
be changed and developed, the teacher provides the
learner with a model of how a writer goes about the
task of editing and revising a draft and seeks to
share his/her expertise with the inexperienced
writer. There are, though, a number of problems
associated with the strategy, despite its advantages of directness and simplicity.

It is possible, for example, for the teacher
to use the 'postal' approach and return a child's
draft not simply 'corrected' (that is, with changes
made to spelling, punctuation and grammatical usage),
but also transformed in more fundamental ways. To
work on a pupil's draft in this way may at first
appear to be an economic and effective way of using
the teacher's time because it is accepted (in
principle at least) that when the script is returned,
the pupil will examine the changes and will understand the reasons for them. The insights that this
process brings, it is hoped, will help the writer
to gain new skills which will be applied to future
tasks. With the majority of pupils, however, this
hope usually proves illusory.

By working on, correcting and improving a child's

draft, it is relatively easy for teachers to ensure that successful written work is eventually produced for display on the walls of the classroom or for inclusion in a folio of writing, but much of the essential labour in achieving this goal will have been done by the teacher, not by the child. Because of pressure of time the teacher has demonstrated to the pupil only a set of possible solutions to problems perceived by the teacher-editor in isolation; the processes that have been worked through to arrive at these solutions (as far as the pupil is concerned) remain hidden. Although the teacher may spend many hours correcting and revising pupils' scripts at home or in staff-room, when the edited drafts come to be returned, the pupils will probably be anxious only to incorporate the changes that have been made into a 'fair copy' and to bring the task to a speedy conclusion. Some teachers may argue in reply that when they take over a child's draft in this way in order to correct and develop it (and perhaps to type it for some form of publication), the final product is still essentially the child's; they have acted, they maintain, merely as editor. But unless any changes made to the text are minimal and superficial, this argument is mistaken. In taking on an editorial role of this kind, the teacher is providing a short-cut in a journey pupils need to make for themselves. Although the teacher may well seek to demonstrate how a pupil's draft can be improved, the actual process of improvement needs to be carried out, in part at least, by the original writer so that the meanings to be communicated in the written text, its vocabulary and language structures, remain under his/her control.

In any case, there is no guarantee that pupils will look with favour on editorial changes made by the teacher without consultation. For example, one boy (Brian) working on the simulated newspaper report described in the previous chapter appears affronted when he discovers a minor mismatch between his own final handwritten draft (which gives an account of how Prince William as an infant received a vaccination against whooping cough) and a typed version for final presentation that he has received from his teacher. In the following classroom extract Brian discusses the offending typescript with Stephen and William who sit next to him:

Teacher	*If you want you can cut that* (the type-script) *out and put it in one of your blank spaces. This is your own ... achievement ...*
Stephen	*Whit's that?* (giving out scripts)
Brian	*Which yin's yours?*
Teacher	*It's a typed version of your report, so if you've got a space somewhere in your work ...*
Brian	*Who done ... 'Flock to Highland Gathering'? ... How did I ken that, eh?*
Teacher	*If you want, you can cut your one out and stick it in there as well.*
William	(reads his own aloud)
Stephen	*Whose is that 'Royal Vaccination'?*
Brian	*Mines ...* (reads his out loud) *... Whit did I write? ... I didna write that!*
William	(reading)*'hoped'*
Brian	*No. I'm talking aboot, I didnae write 'hoped'*
William	*Where is yours?*
Brian	*My good copy? We'll read it out and see if it's the same. Right I'll read this yin out and you follow it there.*
	'The Royal Vaccination ... At Buckingham Palace yesterday Prince William got his whooping-cough jag, em, whooping cough vaccination, when a private nurse and doctor came to the palace in the morning.
	Whooping cough is on the increase at the moment and the royal approval by the Royal Family encourage other people to get it.'
William	*'... and it is hoped'*
Brian	*That's different. A' kent there was something wrong. Whaur was the 'hoped' aboot?*
William	*'... at the moment and it is hoped this will...' You've missed 'and it is hoped.'*
Brian	*Well, where's my rough copy? My rough copy's here. There it's. See it's not got 'hoped' there. Miss, see when you see this and eh, it's not got ...*
(Stephen	*Shut up!)*
Brian	*... it's no got 'hoped' in it ...*
Stephen	*Miss, they're trying to make you seem ba' heidit or ...*
Brian	*'... at the moment and it is hoped that royal approval will encourage other people to get it' And there ... if you see it in my copy ...*
Teacher	*Did you change your rough copy?*

Brian	*No*
Teacher	*Where's your rough copy?*
Brian	*There it is*
Teacher	*Uh huh ... You have*
Brian	*Have I, whaur aboot?*
Teacher	*'... and this will encourage other people to get it.'*
William	*Ah but it's 'hoped'*
Teacher	*Sorry?*
Brian	*It's when it says 'I hoped' I just wondered...*
Teacher	*Oh I put in a 'hoped'. So I have ... Where was it? Ah well you'd have to be- cause it wouldn't make sense the way ... 'whooping cough is on the increase at the moment and this royal approval ... this approval by the Royal Family encourage other people to get it'. Right? It needs a 'hoped'; I must just have done it without thinking because it needs that to make it make sense.*
Brian	*Right*

(Roger 1982b)

Despite her good intentions, in producing a final amended typed version the teacher seems to have offended Brian's view of the integrity of his copy.

A further problem likely to be experienced when the teacher demonstrates ways in which a script can be developed and revised is that even when the teacher seeks to help a pupil orally in a conference the act of showing can be perceived by a child as a definitive solution, not as one of a number of poss- ibilities. The writer believes that the teacher's suggestion has to be taken over and incorporated uncritically into the draft. Again, because of the demands of the classroom and the pressure of limited time, the pupil may not fully understand the nature of the improvement that is being suggested or how and why it has been arrived at. For example, when Brian was working on an earlier draft of the same newspaper report, his teacher read his draft and showed him orally how it could be developed. The intended help, however, creates a dilemma for him which he solves only with difficulty. Brian obviously believes that the teacher's suggested development of his text is conclusive. His problem is that after she has left his desk to work with another pupil, Brian cannot remember the exact wording she had used; the confusion of the words *request* and *inquest* creates special difficulties:

Teacher	*Right, Brian, how's the capital letters getting on?*
Brian	*I'm trying to think of ...*
Teacher	*Why is that a capital?*
Brian	*It was just the way I had writ it*
Teacher	*I know it's the way you'd 'writ' it; you 'writ' it as a capital. It disnae make it right. It should be a small one shouldn't it? You never get a capital letter in the middle of a word, ever ... '... when a private nurse or ...' that should be 'and doctor came to the Palace.' You've already given that a capital. Was it 'This morning, yesterday morning...'? Make it 'yesterday' ...*
	You'll be doing this again; I'm correcting them, and your spelling ... O.K. 'Buckingham Palace'... oh you've got, I beg your pardon, 'Yesterday Prince William got his whooping-cough vaccination when a private nurse and doctor came to the Palace' ... Oh I see what you mean, it's kind of a long way down, isn't it?
Brian	*I was trying to think, I was trying to reverse ...*
Teacher	*Why don't you say, 'Prince William got his whooping-cough vaccination yesterday when a private nurse and doctor came to Buckingham Palace at the request of the royal parents.' You know they make quite a fuss about it because they want to encourage other people to warn about the real danger of it ...* (the teacher moves to another pupil).
Brian	(to Stephen)
Stephen	*A whit?*
Brian	*-quest*
Stephen	*Ask, look ...*
Brian	*I'm no looking it up. I wouldnae ken, I dinnae ken how to spell it; I dinnae even ken the first letter of it. I ken the letter -an, in ... an ...in* (uses a dictionary) ...
	I cannae find it. In ... I cannae find the thing anywhere ...
	I forgot what I was looking for again.
Stephen	*Request*
Brian	*Inquest, aye*
Stephen	*Inquest or request?*
Brian	*Request? ... what did you say?*
Stephen	*The same*

Brian   *In ... I forgot. I'm looking at A ...*
P... I'm trying to think, it's no
'... inquest by the royal family;' I'm
trying to think of the name. I cannae get
it right ...
'inquest' doesnae sound right. 'Cos it
says here ... where is it? 'Legal inquiry
into a case of sudden death.' But ... but
it's no that ...

(Roger 1982b)

Brian never manages to solve his problem satisfactorily; though he identifies the correct word *request,*
the sentence in his final report remains garbled.
    If a teacher is to 'demonstrate success' when
discussing a draft with the writer, it is important
to avoid simply transmitting a series of solutions
to the pupil; ideally an exchange of meanings has to
be negotiated between teacher and writer. Perceived
problems have to be explained; suggested solutions
have to be presented tentatively and discussed.
The 'plans' for writing that exist in the head of
the teacher have to be matched to the 'plans'
already internalised by the pupil. The teacher has
to try to discover what the writer is seeking to
communicate, and to develop this meaning in such a
way that the writer can see the logic of any suggested change and can accept it as a development of the
original purpose and meaning. Such a sensitive and
careful approach is achieved in the reality of the
classroom only with great difficulty. It is not
surprising perhaps that teachers tend to concentrate
on changing obvious surface features of a script or
simply create their own more substantial changes in
a child's text without any explanation or negotia-
tion.
    Alternatively, it is possible for some form of
demonstration to be implemented as a teacher-led
activity with the whole class, not as a strategy for
individual or group work. It is not necessary for
such an approach to follow a traditional didactic
pattern with the teacher lecturing the class. One
teacher, for example, described in interview a
technique he uses in the pre-writing phase to
demonstrate how to compose and organise a first draft,
adopting ideas from the class and building up a text
on an overhead projector slide:

> *You take everything step by step ... As you are*
> *writing the stuff out on the overhead they're*
> *realising that it's not just a big slap-dash*
> *thing, that everything's going slowly and that*
> *you're moving towards things. You end up with*
> *a scribbled outline and then they complete it*
> *according to their own ideas. You're saying,*
> *'By no means is that the story, that's*
> *pointers and guides ...'*
>
> (Peacock and Roger 1984 p.18)

The approach that is outlined here can also be
adopted when pupils have begun to write their own
drafts in response to a task. The teacher can use
one or more scripts to demonstrate how the draft can
be developed and improved, using the overhead
projector with class discussion, teasing out ideas
and suggestions and showing how an experienced
writer can work and re-work a text.

Demonstration techniques do not have to be
dominated by the teacher. They can also require a
high degree of pupil participation. For example,
the following 'fish-bowl activity' aims to demonstrate editorial skills and encourage 'peer
revision' of drafts. The class watch and eventually
discuss a scene improvised by three pupils. Before
the scene is acted out, the class have already
completed a first draft in response to a set assignment, the purpose and context of which have been
explained and discussed. The three selected pupils
are given the roles of the writer of the draft
(which can be genuine), an editor who has to improve
the draft, and a proof-reader. While the scene is
in progress the class watch and listen, noting the
group's comments and how they interact. The scene
is then discussed by teacher and class to draw attention to aspects of the revising and editing process.
If appropriate, the scene can be repeated with three
different participants and the same or a different
text so that what has been learned from the first
observation, discussion and evaluation can be
applied to the second attempt. The teacher can of
course also participate in the scene to act as a
model, but normally when this approach is used the
pupils learn 'on the job' and from each other.
(Christenbury 1982 pp. 120-121)

All of the demonstration activities that have
been described and discussed aim to influence in
some way pupils' own independent efforts when they
come to revise their written work. In completing
an autobiographical task when pupils had to write

their accounts of their own recollected first day at
secondary school for an audience of senior primary
children, the draft of one boy (Joseph) was subjected
to a lively and quite detailed group discussion
which involved both teacher and peers. On that
occasion Joseph finally lost patience and brought
the session to a conclusion, obviously feeling that
he had been given more advice than he could cope
with. But it is interesting to note that soon after-
wards (but at a later date) he offered the following
advice to another pupil, Andrew, when the pair discussed Andrew's draft with a view to improving it:

Andrew	(to Joseph) *Right what do you want me to take oot and put in?*
Joseph	*Right, I would like you where it says 'After filling in our timetables we sat in the class for a period ...' you could say how long a period is because if they hear a bell they could think it's the fire alarm ... Maybe they don't know what the periods are like, so you could say how long the periods are.*
Andrew	*Right, I'll put in how long the periods are, right.*
Joseph	*And there was another one. 'And it was very exciting because everybody was pushing...' Well, maybe it's no exciting to them because they could lose their concentration going up the stairs, like, turning roon, if anybody pushed them they could fall. So you could maybe say some-thing like 'rushing'.*
Andrew	*Aye, 'rushing', right.*
Joseph	*And up here you could put some more inform-ation where it says, 'When we first got into the class we just got used to the teacher and the teacher was taking our names. When the day was over I was very happy. I knew my faither was waiting to give me a run home in the car.' You should maybe gie some more information about what you thought your timetable was, you ken.*
Andrew	*Well, I'll just have to write it out again and put in the things...*
Joseph	*You havenae mentioned your register class-room. You could say what (it is) because they havenae got registration or anything.*
Andrew	*I have so. Aye, 'after we filled in our timetables we sat in the class for a period, then we went to our first class.'*

Joseph   *'We went to our first class', but you never
              said nothing about the 'reggie' because
              they havenae got registration o'er there
              and you could say what it's like...*
                        (Peacock and Roger 1984 p.176)

Joseph's approach to his editorial role is perhaps
too directive in the way he suggests changes and
developments to Andrew's work; he is a little
abrupt in the way he gives his advice. But in other
ways he has been clearly influenced by the earlier
discussion of his own draft. The questions he had
been asked by the teacher and peers on that occasion
and the recommendations that were made for improvements to his own draft have helped him to look
critically, but positively, at the work of another
writer and to offer him advice and practical assistance.

PRACTICE

Creating a unique, extended written text puts many
demands on a young, inexperienced writer. It has
already been argued that practice alone will not help
pupils to overcome their difficulties and improve
as writers. On the other hand, practice clearly has
a part to play in a child's writing development.
After all it is not possible to become a more successful and effective writer unless you are given the
opportunity to engage in the actual activity of
writing. If, for example, teachers choose to
organise classroom work in such a way that pupils
spend most of their time watching, listening and
talking, with only restricted opportunities for reading and writing and even then only as 'short burst'
activities, it should not surprise us if children's
skills and self-confidence as writers do not
increase.
     Writing, it has been argued, should be
conceptualised as a complex totality, not as a set
of separable, discrete skills which can be taught
and mastered in isolation. But this does not
signify that practice directed to a particular aspect
of writing is necessarily unhelpful. If such
practice can be set within the context of a clearly
defined writing task so that the inexperienced
writer moves from the main problem of communicating
a total message in written form to one particular
aspect of it and then back again to the total
communicative context, this concentration on one
feature (or a limited combination of features) can

be beneficial. Practice in specific skills in
writing can be made worthwhile, provided that the
writers concerned can see the need for such practice
and understand how it relates to their development
as writers. Conversely, if practice in writing
skills is perceived by pupils as an isolated activity
without much purpose or point, it will probably have
little lasting effect. A key problem, then, that
you have to solve as a teacher is how to provide
writing practice in the classroom that is both meaningful and purposeful in the eyes of your pupils.

For example, most teachers of writing now seem
to accept (in principle, if not always in practice)
that the traditional strategy of children writing
out their spelling 'corrections' a certain number
of times is often a demoralising waste of time for
both teacher and pupil. The strategy ensures that
pupils copy out as a retrospective exercise a
selection of mis-spelled words that the teacher has
identified in their scripts. Usually the teacher
either demonstrates the correct spelling in the
margin of the pupil's text (as in the case of
Adele's teacher) or attention is drawn to particular
words so that the pupil can check for the correct
spelling in a dictionary or word list. Whichever
approach is adopted, the act of copying aims to
help the writer to identify and remember the correct
spelling of the words in question. In effect the
pupil often simply lists the selected words as an
unreflecting copying exercise. The sequence of
letters is soon forgotten and the same errors often
reappear at a later date. The writing of spelling
corrections thus becomes a mechanical chore which
pupils carry out as a decontextualised task often
long after their original drafts were written.

The traditional dictation exercise, on the
other hand, in which the teacher narrates a short
text aloud for the pupils to transcribe, does help
pupils to concentrate their attention on the
problems of translating an aural text into a written
one. In completing a dictation task pupils do not
have to cope with the problem of composing and
organising their own meanings; they have simply to
hold in short-term memory a limited unit of meaningful text and transcribe it accurately. Dictation
exercises of this kind, whether they are oral/aural
for a large group or taped for individual practice,
obviously are intended to give practice in transcription skills. However, they can also help pupils to
develop an awareness of any discrepancies that may
exist between their own pronunciation of words and

the models of pronunciation on which the spelling
of most words is based. Pupils hear written texts
spoken aloud by the teacher using a form of standard,
received pronunciation and they have to translate
these sounds into correctly spelled words.
(Shaughnessy 1977 p.179) This can be a helpful
strategy for many pupils, because although all poor
spellers experience difficulty in the visual recall
of words, in many cases a child's problem may also
involve the additional problem of auditory discrimination and recall.(Cotterell 1974)
   The strategy of oral dictation can also be
adapted to develop pupils' awareness of skills in
revising a composed text. In this case pupils are
not required to reproduce a text dictated by the
teacher, but to edit it silently in their heads
before transcribing it. The text (one of the pupil's
own drafts, for example) is read aloud to the class
in its entirety so that its total meaning is conveyed.
It is then read by the teacher a second time, sentence
by sentence, as in a dictation exercise. However, at
the conclusion of each sentence the class is told to
make a specified change to the text - to make it
longer or shorter, for example, more detailed or less
complex. Pupils have to make the required change
silently in their heads within a given limited
period of time before writing it down. When the
task has been completed, the different changes made
by the class (and by the teacher) form the subject-
matter for discussion. The focus for such discussion
is not the accuracy of the transcription but the
nature of the revisions that pupils have made to the
text. (Scardamalia *et al* 1981 pp.161-162)
   Practice can also be directed to the clarity
and explicitness of a writer's message. In 'the
map game', for example, this quest for clarity and
explicitness is achieved orally as a pre-writing
activity. Pupils work in pairs; they are given
copies of a local street map or school plan, together
with teacher-prepared cards which state a variety
of starting-points and destinations. Each pupil
explains in turn to his/her partner how to get from
the prescribed starting-point to the destination
without actually stating what the goal is. The
speaker is allowed no questions or prompts from the
listener but both are allowed a pen or pencil to
trace the route; it has to be assumed that the
listener has no local knowledge. The game ends when
the speaker says, 'You are now at your destination
- where are you?' If the listener's reply is incorrect, the speaker must try again. The game (and

other similar tasks that can be developed from it)
prepares the way for pupils to attempt to write
their own clear accurate directions or instructions
with the further aim of testing out these directions
in practice. (Onion 1976 p.5)

A similar, related activity can be adopted after
writers have completed a draft. Pupils take turns
in reading aloud to their peers, either their own
scripts or scripts provided by the teacher, working
again in pairs or in small groups. After an initial
reading to convey the total impression of the piece,
the writer reads the text a second time more slowly.
On this occasion the listeners are encouraged to
interrupt, to be deliberately awkward in misinterpret-
ing the meaning, and to demand more information. The
reader must respond to these interruptions immediately by writing additions to the text to improve its
clarity. In this way (as in the earlier reproduced
editorial discussion between Joseph and Andrew) the
writer is helped to become more sensitive to what
he/she takes for granted when composing a draft and
the ways in which the intended meaning can be made
more lucid and explicit for a reader who does not
share the same knowledge and assumptions. (Bartz
1976 pp.92-94)

None of these selected strategies designed to
give practice in writing is foolproof. Their
success in the classroom will depend on how the
teacher uses them, how they are related to the
writing problems children are actually experiencing
and how they are perceived by pupils. In the right
circumstances, though, the strategies that have been
described (and others like them) can assist the
development of pupils' understanding of the nature
of written communication and increase their skills
in creating their own extended scripts.

DISCRIMINATING

In the previous chapter it was argued that a written
model should be used at the pre-writing stage to help
pupils to identify what was likely to count as a
successful outcome before they begin to work on their
own drafts. It was argued too that a model could be
one source of help while pupils were actually
engaged on the writing task or when they discussed
their work with teacher or peers; the model could be
referred to as exemplification or as a resource to
stimulate ideas. A central purpose, then, in the
classroom use of a written model would be to enable
pupils to discriminate more confidently and explicitly

between degrees of perceived success. Although the processes of developing discrimination can be assisted initially by the teacher, the long-term aim would obviously be for pupils to achieve complete independence in making judgements about their progress towards success in completing a task.
     The overall strategy of 'discrimination training' aims to help pupils to distinguish in varied contexts between a 'target' of success and some kind of unsatisfactory 'foil'. In using this strategy in the teaching of writing, therefore, children are helped to discriminate between a success-ful and unsuccessful written outcome.
     Initially this can be achieved in a fairly broad and general way, but as they gain increasing experience and knowledge children can become more perceptive and articulate about the constituent elements of success and failure. Advocates of the strategy argue that in order to 'shape' their own performance as they work on a task, learners must first gain confidence about what a good performance looks like and what is wrong with a poor one. In other words appropriate standards have to be gradual-ly learned for evaluating a written performance. Examining adequate and inadequate examples of writing and becoming more aware of the differences between them helps children to internalise these standards and apply them to their own writing. (Smith D.E.P. *et al* 1976 Volume 1 p.119)
     The acquisition of such internalised standards is obviously a long, and complex process; they are not simply transmitted in the classroom by a single teacher and learned overnight. However, teachers can make a continuing contribution to help children to acquire what they (the teachers) perceive to be appropriate standards for the successful completion of written work and this process can begin for pupils from an early age. In this way they can become gradually more independent in the judgements they make, more able to monitor their own progress on a task, and increasingly aware of how close or how far they are from the goals that have been set.
     The ability to discriminate between some kind of target model and foil, between degrees of success and failure in writing, is clearly an important characteristic of the independent writer; essential skills are acquired and refined gradually over a long period of time and this process of development can be life-long. The teacher's ultimate goal, therefore, would be for appropriate models of different kinds of writing to become part of a set

of internalised 'plans' which exist within the mind of the writer. Initially, though, as we argued in Chapter Five, appropriate models can be provided in a more concrete form in the classroom and some of the constituent elements of each model can be made explicit and clarified by different kinds of class-room activity. Eventually most pupils will begin to make independent judgements of different kinds as they write and become increasingly aware of different kinds of discrepancy that exist between the foils they themselves produce as they work on their drafts and the models of success that are internalised in their imagination. Until this point of confident independence is reached, however, teachers can help pupils to make progress towards it by making these discrepancies more visible and explicit.

In using a written model in the classroom, the teacher is again not obliged to adopt a traditional didactic teaching style and explain to the whole class why the model is successful. The approach can be more indirect and inductive. the teacher can, for example, withhold the introduction of a model until after the pupils have completed their own first drafts. In this way the exemplar does not have an undue influence as pupils begin to write; there is less pressure on the writer to 'please the teacher' by simply reproducing what has been recommended. An illustration of this strategy in practice can be taken from a small unit of classroom work which involved a (second) simulated newspaper report to be entitled 'Rescue Groups Ease the Crisis' (derived from Shuman 1975 pp.75-77).

The context of the task was a period of except-ionally cold weather during which the local commun-ity had experienced a variety of serious, related problems - freezing pipes, for example, icy pave-ments and roads blocked by snow. Pre-writing preparation included discussion about the hardships people were suffering during the freezing conditions, which particular groups were most at risk, and the sources of help that were being provided. The discussion was led by the teacher and closely related to what pupils themselves had experienced or witnessed in the neighbourhood or had seen on television news reports. As this exchange of ideas progressed, the teacher summarised it on the black-board under different headings. Each pupil then drew up a preparatory list of those groups of people that were most likely to need some kind of help and those groups that were likely to provide it. In addition the teacher gave the class a list of ten key words that had to be included at some point in their reports. These words could be changed slightly, if the writer wished, and could be used in any order. Once this phase was over, the class proceeded to write their own first drafts. One example of such a draft together with the writer's plan and the list of key words is reproduced as Figure 6.2.

It was only after pupils had reached this point, when their first drafts had been completed, that the teacher introduced a written model to exemplify success on the task. The model (reproduced as Appendix A) took the form of an article from a local newspaper with the same title (pre-selected by the teacher for that reason) and it dealt with the same subject-matter as the pupils' own draft reports. The article also contained the ten key words the pupils had already been given. The teacher read the model and asked the class to compare it with their own draft reports - in what ways was the newspaper report different from their own? was it better? if so why?

At first pupils seemed anxious to identify the ten key words in the article and it is arguable that this aspect of the approach was again counter-productive in constraining the pupils' own writing and diverting attention from more important matters. None the less the recent experience of struggling with the problems of writing their own draft reports on the subject seemed to motivate the class to examine the article with increased care and interest. They seemed more alert to the different kinds of information the professional writer had included and the style she had adopted than would have been the case in a more cursory reading.

After reading and informally discussing the article, pupils were then given a variation in their normal classroom redrafting procedure. Instead of continuing to work on their own scripts, the teacher arranged for each pupil to be given the draft of another pupil. In the light of what had been learned from the model (but without copying it directly) they had to edit and improve this draft rather than their own. Once this task was completed the final edited report was returned to the original writer for further examination and discussion. So, in the course of completing the different stages of the total task, each writer had been made more aware of a variety of differences between his/her first draft, the target model and the second draft revised by another pupil.

60229957

```
RESCUE GROUPS EASE THE CRISIS

NEEDED HELP              HELPING

Burst Pipes             Plumber,Council
Floods                  Plumber,Council,Army,RAF
Sheep,Cattle,Farmers    RAF
Icy Roads               Council
Power Cuts              Electricity Board
Schools                 Plumber,Council
Runways                 Snow-plough

Temperature, tennants, response, estimated,
emergency, colleagues, contribution,
temporary, handicapped, depended.

Today temperatures were recorded at the lowest
peak ever since 1880.
Emergency services had to be called in to help
the handicapped find temporary housing, due to
severe floods.  Damages are estimated over
£2.5 million pounds.  Tennants have shown great
response in putting up some of the handicapped
up.  The JP for - Mr David - of - District
Council said that these people have depended
on getting temporary accomodation.  We would
urge the people of - to add a small contribut-
ion.
```

Figure 6.2 'Rescue Groups Ease The Crisis':
Pupil's plan and first draft

A written model can be a complex and flexible
teaching resource; its varied features can be used
for different kinds of comparison and they can be
related to a variety of different problems experienced by individual children. It is possible,
though, for the teacher to move away from this more
general approach and direct a pupil's attention to
a specific aspect of a draft and help the writer to
discriminate more accurately between success and
failure in a limited field. Accuracy of spelling is
an obvious example of such a focusing technique.

Inexperienced writers inevitably produce their own spelling foils in the form of misspelled words and the target models available for comparison in dictionaries and word lists are normally permanent and precise. The writer's perception of the differences between the correct and incorrect forms can be made more acute in a variety of ways. The word can be broken down into more manageable visual units and the 'hard spots' emphasised; letter order can be reinforced by naming the letters alphabetically; the word can be 'sounded out' or enunciated aloud to highlight essential written letters which are not anticipated in the oral pronunciation of the word; and if necessary letter shapes can be traced with finger or pencil. To test that a word is fixed in short-term memory, the correct spelling is not simply copied; it is written from memory and then compared with the target model until the version written by the learner matches the model exactly (Cotterell 1974 pp.52-53, Moorhouse 1977 p.16). No strategy is likely to provide a definitive solution to pupils' spelling difficulties, but the approaches that have been described are more likely to help a child to grow in confidence and skill as a speller than constant unreflecting practice.

SOLVING PROBLEMS

Although children should be given the opportunity to practice skills in writing, this need not imply an element of drudgery for the writers. It is not necessary to conjure up a picture of children engaged in the unreflecting repetition of routines and the completion of textbook exercises. Discussion elsewhere in this chapter has shown that this need not be the case, especially when the teacher plans for some element of problem-solving, simulation or play to be included when a writing skill is practised.

A problem-solving approach in the classroom can provide a powerful and positive source of intrinsic motivation for pupils' work. If a child is purposefully engaged in a self-chosen task and encounters a problem that frustrates its completion, then he/she is normally strongly motivated towards overcoming the problem, provided that the eventual goal is of sufficient importance and the problem encountered is not intractable. Most teachers recognise the power of pupils' intrinsic motivation and seek to stimulate interest in their classrooms so that this power can be released. It is one reason why pre-writing activities are of such importance, for it is during this phase in the classroom, when the task is introduced and its nature and purpose explained, that pupils' interest and involvement are won. However, most teachers will probably agree that it is unrealistic to rely totally on this source of motivation and to expect all children to be personally committed to their classroom work all the time. None the less, it is still possible for teachers to adopt a problem-solving approach when they plan a unit of classroom work. The problems that are created in this way may be fabricated by the teacher for his/her own purposes rather than derived from the pupils' own 'genuine' interests and concerns, but the strategy seeks to engage the children in a classroom task and ensure their active involvement in its completion.

A problem-solving approach can be successfully applied to various aspects of the teaching of writing. A simple example which helps to distinguish between the different kinds of strategy that have so far been described would be an occasion when a teacher is asked for the spelling of a particular word when a child is writing a first draft. In such a context the teacher could simply demonstrate the correct spelling; this would entail the teacher writing the word on a piece of scrap paper and the pupil would then copy it into his/her own text and perhaps include in in a personal dictionary for future practice. On the other hand, the teacher could encourage the pupil to discriminate between the foil that the writer has produced in the draft and the model that has been demonstrated. Or, thirdly, the teacher could insist that the writer solves the problem alone (or with some kind of limited assistance) by looking the word up in a dictionary. This final course of action would almost certainly be the most time-consuming for most pupils (especially if they are also encouraged to apply some kind of discrimination learning to the word when it has been found), but the long-term benefits of the strategy could be increased confidence and skill in using a dictionary for reference and related research skills, increased independence from the teacher and (perhaps) more effective and permament learning.

The proof-reading and editing of other writers' drafts can also be presented to a class as a problem-solving exercise. If pupils understand the nature and purpose of what is to be communicated, they can become actively involved in the close reading of a script both to check for errors and to improve its

clarity and style. (Shaughnessy 1977 pp.222-223)
Proof-reading can even be organised by the teacher
as a competitive activity with pupils checking drafts
for a specified number of different kinds of error.
These deliberate mistakes can either be created by
the teacher or by the pupils themselves working in
pairs.(Scardamalia *et al* 1981 p.93)   Proof-reading
exercises help children to look at a written script
dispassionately and objectively. They help them to
become more alert to different aspects of the writing
process and to features of the script they have
examined simply because they are remote from its
composition and creation. Inexperienced writers can
gradually come to view a written script from the
reader's perspective and shift their own self-
centred point of view. As was argued in earlier
chapters, the young writer's own subjectivity can be
a fundamental obstacle to progress. Children tend to
take for granted the clarity of the message they are
trying to communicate and to miss seeing what they
have in fact written (or failed to write). The
editing of other people's drafts can help them to
accept the importance of the 'disinterested watch-
fulness' that a skilled writer takes for granted
and to apply it to their own work when they write,
review and revise. (Shaughnessy 1977 p.182)
     In a similar way a problem-solving approach can
help pupils to understand better the need for
punctuation in a written text. Most teachers of
writing understandably grow tired of explaining and
demonstrating the rules and conventions of punctuation, of prescribing practice in its uses in the
form of conventional exercises, of trying to persuade
children to discriminate between appropriate and
inappropriate uses, because these strategies do not
appear to exert much influence on the ways in which
pupils insert (or fail to insert) punctuation marks
when they write their own extended drafts. Again
the problems pupils experience in using punctuation
signals seem to be caused in part by the writer's
own subjectivity and in part by their confusion
about the principles that underpin punctuation.
Many children do not anticipate any likely difficulties for a reader in comprehending and interpreting
the intended written message. When inexperienced
writers compose and review a draft, the patterns of
intonation and meaning and the grammatical structures
of the text may appear self-evidently clear to them.
In addition the rules of punctuation may not have
been fully grasped so that signals and markers are
used inappropriately or not at all. Unless children

can be helped to see the need for punctuation when they write and to understand the principles which underlie its different forms, little significant progress is likely to be made in this field.

Such increased awareness and improved understanding of the logic of punctuation may be achieved more successfully by problem-solving approaches rather than by more traditional methods. Pupils can work in pairs trying to read aloud at sight specially prepared texts that are either unpunctuated or are distorted by inappropriate punctuation. They can exchange their own drafts and examine them for punctuation errors, making out a case for essential changes. (Shaughnessy 1977 p.39) Instead of learning punctuation rules merely from a teacher's explanation or from a textbook, children can be given the task of writing their own rules for one or more of the conventions of punctuation.

For example, a class can be given a prepared text which is set out without punctuation of any kind or with one important feature of punctuation omitted. Pupils then have to write a specified punctuation rule in their own words for the benefit of other pupils who will have to insert the appropriate mark in the text. The rule that is drafted can be tested out against any written evidence available in the classroom or by a peer and the explanation has to be clear enough for a writer to be able to insert the necessary mark in the given text with confidence. The pupil testing out the rule can be as uncooperative in interpreting the explanation as he/she wishes. In their attempts to draft a given rule pupils are permitted, therefore, to refer to any source of print that is available in the classroom except a grammar textbook where the rule is explained and exemplified. In other words, in their search for an adequate and clear statement, pupils may examine different kinds of text to investigate when and why a particular punctuation signal is actually used in different printed texts. Rules for punctuation are thus reached by means of inductive inquiry rather than accepted because of an authoritative explanation from teacher or textbook.

To conclude, then, we have argued in the course of this chapter that there are no strategies in the teaching of writing that in themselves ensure that all children will learn effectively, that guarantee that pupils will overcome their difficulties and develop necessary skills. The different kinds of strategy that have been described, exemplified and discussed, have been presented with a view to

teachers exploiting all or some of them in the
context of their own classroom work; these approaches
and examples can obviously be adapted to suit different contexts and purposes. Some strategies will
be selected rather than others because of a teacher's
preferred style of teaching; equally some rather
than others will be preferred by pupils because of
their own individual learning styles. And success
will not be brought about simply by using a particular strategy in isolation. Success and progress in
writing will inevitably depend also on the climate
for learning that has been established in school and
classroom, the nature of the relationships that
exist there, the professional skills of the teacher,
and the selected strategy being embedded in a meaningful and purposeful context of classroom work.

However, it is of particular interest in the
present discussion that two independent researchers
have recently emphasised the importance of a problem-
solving approach in the teaching of writing.
Arthur Applebee comments in his research report
on the teaching of writing in American High Schools
that one important feature of the agreed 'best
observed lessons' was students being faced 'with
problems that had to be solved out of their own
intellectual and experiential resources' (Applebee
1981 p.105). And similarly, in a research review
to discover which classroom approaches appear to be
most effective in the teaching of writing, George
Hillocks also comments on the apparent importance
of a mode of teaching which is characterised by
high levels of pupil interaction in problem-centred
discussion. This appears to be especially the case
when the problems have been selected by the teacher
'to engage students with each other in specifiable
processes important to some aspect of writing'
(Hillocks 1984 pp.144-146). Problem-solving
strategies may therefore be of particular importance
in the classroom both in order to win pupils'
positive motivation, and, especially, to promote
their development and growth as writers.

Chapter Seven

SUCCESS IN WRITING: THEORY AND PRACTICE

The different proposals concerning the teaching of
writing that have been discussed and illustrated in
the course of the preceding chapters are now brought
together to form the basis of a coherent theoretical
rationale for the teaching of writing in schools.
This theoretical statement is then exemplified by a
classroom case study to show how the proposed
rationale can be implemented in practice. Finally
in the concluding chapter we consider the changes
in professional thinking and classroom methods
that would be necessary if the rationale were to be
more widely accepted and implemented in schools.
     The proposed rationale would have two main aims:
first, to enable the great majority of pupils in our
schools to experience a greater sense of achievement
in their progress as writers than is at present the
case; and second, to ensure that in the course of
their attempts to master different modes of writing
children become increasingly aware in their classroom work of those qualities that are essential to
the attainment of success.
     Clearly the achievement of continuing and varied
success in writing will not depend on one aspect of
classroom practice alone, but on a number of important inter-related features - the knowledge and
professional skills of the teacher, the choice of
appropriate goals and materials, the 'climate for
learning' established in the classroom, and appropriate assessment procedures designed to provide
effective feedback and a valid and reliable evaluation of success. The classroom methodology that is
being proposed, therefore, seeks to take account of
this complex totality and to provide guidelines for
its implementation that are sufficiently flexible
and adaptable to enable the methodology to be
exploited by different teachers working in a variety

of educational contexts.

Of central importance to the proposed rationale, however, is pupils' achievement of visible success in writing. It is to this concept, therefore, and the clarification of its meaning that we first turn our attention.

THE CONCEPT OF SUCCESS

Throughout our discussion of the teaching of writing we have accepted the importance of pupils' producing extended writing in their own words, rather than 'short-burst' answers written in response to a text-book or worksheet exercise, or copy-book imitations of other writers' work. Few experienced writers, however, are ever completely satisfied that their final drafts are totally successful. Nor is it possible to draw an agreed, clearly defined line between a successful and an unsuccessful written product. Most of the written texts we create usually contain some features that we regard as acceptable, while other aspects often appear less satisfactory. The achievement of success in writing, in a sense, remains a continuing ambition which is never fully realised. We continue to develop skills over a long period of time and these skills relate to different modes of writing. The modes themselves are appropriate to different purposes and audiences, and skill in using them involves the mastery of a range of conventions appropriate to different kinds of written text.

As indicated in Chapter Two, it is possible to 'map' the whole domain of extended writing, categor-ising it in terms of different modes or genres and to develop these categories in more detail accord-ing to purpose and audience. And it is possible, too, to categorise writing in terms of the skills that have to be acquired or the conventions that have to be mastered by a beginning writer. (Smith D.E.P. *et al* 1977 (Volume 2) p.13; Roberts 1979 pp. 28-29) But for our present purpose neither approach is completely satisfactory. The mastery of grapho-logical conventions is not in itself important. These conventions become important only when applied to a written communication in a particular context and for a defined audience. And there are no agreed levels of achievement which represent the point at which a child may be designated a 'successful' writer of narrative fiction, for example, but as yet an 'unsuccessful' writer of argumentative prose.

A map of the whole domain of writing is import-

ant and helpful in that it makes us more aware of the
complexity of the different writing purposes and outcomes that are possible in the classroom and it can
provide us with a comprehensive curriculum for the
teaching of writing. Such a curriculum would ensure
that a variety of modes of writing or genres are
taught in the course of a child's education and that
these modes are addressed to a variety of audiences.
In implementing the curriculum, teachers would
organise classroom work either as a sequential progression, structured according to the perceived
difficulty of each selected mode or genre, or
alternatively, as a continuing 'spiral', with writing
in each designated genre being experienced from an
early stage in a child's education and re-experienced
in a different context at successive later stages.
If the sequential approach is adopted, the teaching
of narrative writing, for example, would probably
precede description, exposition and argument; in the
'spiral' approach, on the other hand, development in
writing would be planned by the school as 'an alter-
nating, interlocking pathway' along which skills
surface, then disappear while new skills are mastered,
and then reappear again later in more complex forms.
(Smith D.E.P. *et al* 1977 (Volume 2) pp.136-137)
Every mode of writing in this latter case would be
experienced by children in a simple form from an
early point in their school careers.

Can there, then, be any stage in their schooling
at which children can be justifiably described as
having achieved success in writing? If so, what
would be the basis of such success? I myself
believe that it is more appropriate and helpful for
the teacher to think, not in terms of pupils mastering decontextualised skills and conventions, or of
writing successfully in a particular genre or mode,
but in terms of the success they achieve in completing specific, but varied writing tasks.

If this approach is adopted, the task becomes
the focus of our attention. A teacher (or group of
teachers) would plan in the course of a school session
different schemes of work which would include as
principal goals key writing tasks to be completed
by all pupils. These tasks would cover a variety of
communicative purposes, set in different contexts
and directed towards different audiences, so that
over an extended period of time the whole domain
of writing could be covered. Work could be planned
either as a sequential progression or as a continuing
'spiral' (depending on how the writing curriculum
was conceptualised by school or department).

The long-term aim of such a writing curriculum would be to help children to make progress towards the ultimate goal of their eventually becoming versatile and successful writers with a varied repertoire of skills. However, in order to promote this long-term development, the teacher's more immediate objective in planning classroom work would be to ensure that each pupil could demonstrate that a particular writing task in a selected mode at an appropriate level of difficulty had been successfully completed. For pupils to achieve this objective, help and support of different kinds could, of course, be provided by the teacher; it would not be essential for the learner to demonstrate that success had been achieved independently, as in a test or examination.

As earlier discussion made clear, success in completing a task would not be evaluated simply as a retrospective exercise. The teacher would need to define the nature of a writing task as clearly as possible *before* pupils began to work on their first drafts and to make explicit to them what is likely to be taken into account when their work is completed and evaluated. As we argued earlier, this strategy does not in itself encourage a more convergent approach to classroom work or an increased emphasis on the teacher's role as 'examiner' when scripts are assessed. It does, however, require teachers to share more explicitly with their pupils their own implicit knowledge and understanding of the nature of the writing process. The teacher has to be prepared to communicate to pupils which features of a written script are perceived as being important or crucial to eventual success. Success on a task does not have to be complete or absolute; the teacher simply needs to make clear what standards of perform-ance will be applied for the task to be accepted as being satisfactorily completed.

If the teacher's criteria for success *are* made clear to pupils at the pre-writing stage (and if, as argued, some form of checklist and model exempli-fying success are provided), pupils can often as a result work in the classroom with greater confidence and independence; they can 'shape' and evaluate their performance on the task and monitor their own and each other's progress more effectively. As we indicated in Chapter Five, the demands a teacher places on a young, inexperienced writer must be realistic. It is not difficult to present children with a checklist that is so detailed that it becomes more of a burden than a support. Any checklist, therefore, should be reasonably brief, containing only those features that are perceived by the teacher as being of greatest importance for the successful completion of the task, and guidelines should be communicated to pupils in a concise, accessible form.

If this approach to the conceptualisation of success is adopted it would not be possible for a teacher to claim at the conclusion of a course or school session that their pupils had 'mastered' narrative writing or that they could now spell or punctuate accurately - because such a claim can never be justified. But it would instead be feasible to present individual profiles of pupils' achievements designed to specify which tasks in a potentially wide communicative field had been successfully completed and the level of difficulty at which they had been attempted. It would also be possible to provide evidence to support these judgements from individual folios of pupils' classroom work. Children's achievements would be visible and explicit; teachers would be able to show that their pupils were making demonstrable progress and were on their way to becoming successful writers.

CLASSROOM METHODOLOGY

The classroom methodology that is being proposed to help children to become more successful writers and has already been illustrated and discussed in more practical terms in preceding chapters, does not pre-suppose a particular style of teaching. As the previous chapter made clear, flexibility in organis-ing and managing the classroom and variety in the choice of teaching methods are acknowledged to be key attributes in the teacher's successful classroom role. *Flexibility* is seen to be important in the way the work of the classroom is planned and managed so that pupils can proceed (individually or in groups) with a range of tasks, working, if approp-riate, at different levels of difficulty and at diff-erent speeds. *Variety* in the selection of learning strategies is also necessary to help children to overcome any difficulties that have been identified by catering for a diversity of learning styles.

A third factor, though, in addition to flexi-bility of management and the selection of varied approaches to teaching, is also seen to be essential to the proposed classroom methodology. This is the creation of adequate time in the classroom (or else-where) to give every pupil the opportunity to draft and redraft their work and complete an appropriate main task successfully. Because children clearly work at different speeds, the creation of *adequate time* will itself presuppose flexibility of classroom management, and the planning of a variety of supporting activities in addition to the main writing assignment. In this way pupils who work quickly, confidently and accurately can be given relevant additional tasks, while further time is allowed (and assistance given) to those children who work and learn more slowly. A single main writing assignment does not require the whole class to progress 'in lock step' and to work at the same level of difficulty.

In other words, and in more practical terms, when teachers prepare a unit of classroom work, they will need to organise a varied context of related activities which are directed towards and support the pupils' main focus of interest - the writing task which is to be undertaken by all pupils. This supporting context will help to prepare the way for the successful completion of the main writing assignment. But in order to allow pupils of different abilities and aptitudes to make progress towards the successful completion of the main task at different speeds the teacher needs to plan additional 'extension' tasks which more able or faster-working pupils can select for further relevant activity. On occasions the teacher will need to deal with the whole class for explanation, questioning and discussion. More often, though, pupils are likely to be working in small groups or on their own, with the teacher informally monitoring their progress and working with individuals or groups, helping to sort out problems and to give advice.

If a class is taught as a single unit with every child expected to proceed at the same pace, success is unlikely to be achieved by all its members, even when the class is organised in a 'set' or 'section' selected according to pupils' perceived abilities and levels of attainment. A minority of children will probably experience some frustration and perform with modest success, and the rest will fail. In fact many teachers seem to approach their classroom work in the expectation that a sizeable proportion of their pupils will fail or at best only partially succeed.

Alternatively, especially when working with unstreamed, all-ability classes, it is possible for teachers to adopt an approach to the teaching of writing that is so open and undefined in its objectives, that at the conclusion of a scheme of work, it is difficult for either teacher or pupils to offer

a confident evaluation of what has been taught or
learned as a result of the classroom activities.
Children are encouraged and stimulated by the
teacher; they select their own learning goals and
activities. And, as a result, the outcomes are often
prolific but confused.

In contrast the rationale that is being proposed
anticipates that teachers who implement it will
accept that it is important and helpful to formulate
and communicate clear, attainable goals in the
teaching of writing and that they themselves will
have an explicit instructional role in the classroom
to help their pupils achieve these goals.

If it is accepted (and clearly such an acceptance cannot be assumed) that in the main it is the
teacher's responsibility to plan and manage a framework of classroom activities and formulate clear
goals when setting a writing task, pupils need not
as a result lack initiative or choice in the
completion of classroom work. Exemplification and
discussion in earlier chapters have shown that their
role in learning is far from passive; they can
interpret tasks in a variety of ways and work with
a large measure of independence. In fact there is
nothing to prevent older pupils themselves being
involved in the creation of a unit of work, in the
specification of aims for a task, or in evaluating
their own success in completing it. Independence
in learning and self-evaluation are obviously
important long-term goals for all pupils.

Any scheme of classroom work, though, will
clearly be partly dependent on pupils' interest
and motivation, on a favourable 'climate for learning' having already been established in classroom
and school, on the relationships built up between
teacher and taught, and on the interest and satisfaction that have been created by previous schemes
of classroom work. If these demanding conditions
can be achieved, then varied pre-writing activities
(such as those described in Chapter Five) can
strengthen classroom motivation, because these
preparatory activities help pupils to understand
better the purpose of an assignment, its context
and audience. If, in addition, some of these pre-
writing activities are also problem-solving in
approach with pupils actively involved in discussion
and inquiry, interest and motivation are likely to be
further increased. But this intrinsic interest can
be strengthened by a further important source of
motivation.

The achievement of success can itself be an

important mainspring. When pupils recognise what they have achieved, that they have made clear progress in the course of completing a task, and are beginning to overcome their difficulties, the experience of success is likely to make a positive impact on morale and on each child's self-concept as a learner. Provided that the tasks pupils are set are appropriate and provided that sufficient time is allowed and adequate help is available, every child should be able to experience some satisfaction of success, no matter how modest their achievements may appear or how limited their scale. In this way the achievement of success becomes an important source of positive motivation. Success encourages further success and influences the child's attitudes to new classroom tasks; self-confidence and self-esteem grow.

Assessment has an important part to play in this process of continuing achievement. It provides essential feedback to the learner about what has been successfully achieved and what still remains to be done. Assessment is therefore a positive experience for the pupils and becomes an integral part of teaching and learning. It does not take the sole form of a concluding evaluation of what the pupil has written; it is partly diagnostic and formative in nature and partly summative. In other words, assessment is designed most importantly to help the learner to identify strengths and weaknesses in an initial or subsequent draft and to help him/her overcome selected difficulties. In this way pupils are assisted in their progress towards the successful completion of the set writing task. A further subsidiary purpose is to evaluate and record the eventual achievement of success.

When they make this final evaluation, teachers will need to base their judgements on the standards which have already been made explicit; both teacher and writer recognise what essential qualities are being looked for in a script. Pupils do not have to guess what lies in the head of the assessor; if the final draft meets the predetermined criteria for success, the script will be accepted as satisfactory. Marks and grades are unnecessary. Pupils are not compared with each other when their final drafts are assessed; performance is evaluated solely against the criteria set for the task. A script is either judged to be satisfactory and success can be recorded, or further work remains to be done.

The traditional approach to the classroom

assessment of writing is quite different; it is
norm-referenced. In evaluating a written script
the teacher uses an implicit internalised model of a
satisfactory or even ideal completion of the task
that has been set. The performance of each pupil
whose work is being assessed is then judged against
this template or blueprint. Probably no pupil will
meet the standards set, because they are so high, and
under normal circumstances no script is awarded A+
or 20/20. Instead a range of marks and grades are
distributed to pupils according to how successfully
(or unsuccessfully) each writer's script matches
the ideal model held in the mind of the assessor.
A few pupils may achieve grade A or 18/20; the
majority will achieve moderate success and get by;
some will fail. Marks between 8 and 14/20 are
acceptable scores; B- or C+ are satisfactory grades.
Different pupils may, of course, be awarded the same
final mark or overall grade for a piece of work, but,
in achieving this standard, the writers may (without realising it) have successfully met different
kinds of criteria.
      It is possible (and now widely practised) to
retain the outcomes of a norm-referenced approach to
assessment - the differential marks or grades -
but to seek to make clearer and more explicit the
criteria which have been used in reaching the
relevant judgements. In this way the criteria that
are adopted are more open to scrutiny and discussion
than is the case when they remain implicit, as in
the traditional approach to the assessment of
pupils' work. But the procedure remains essentially
norm-referenced, not (as some maintain) criterion-
referenced. The final outcome is that children
continue to be separated out and placed in a rank
order so that some are designated 'normal' in their
achievements, while others are above or below the
norm.
      In contrast, the methodology that is being
proposed implements a 'genuine' criterion-referenced
approach to assessment. Criteria for success are
established before the first draft is attempted.
If a pupil completes the assignment and meets these
criteria, then success has been achieved. An
acceptable performance is approved and recorded by
the assessor. Criterion-referenced assessment
accepts an 'all or nothing' approach. Children do
not achieve different degrees of success; their work
is either satisfactory or unsatisfactory. A pupil's
continuing progress is judged according to his/her
achievements in the completion of a series of tasks

with performance evaluated against predetermined and explicit criteria for success. Over a period of time pupils can accumulate 'credits' for their achievements on a variety of tasks at different levels of difficulty; a continuing assessment profile based on these individual achievements can be gradually built up. Assessment is not therefore implemented as a retrospective exercise nor is it competitive in nature; it is an essential part of the total sequence of teaching and learning for each pupil and is integrated into the work of the classroom.

The constituent elements of the proposed classroom rationale are summarised in Figure 7.1 (derived from Bloom 1976 p.11). And the sequence of classroom activities which leads to the achievement of success on a single writing task and its being recorded on an individual assessment profile is represented in Figure 7.2.

CASE STUDY: 'FIRST DAY AT SECONDARY SCHOOL'

The abstract rationale for the teaching of writing that has been described may appear to some readers to be remote from the realities of the classroom. Most teachers are intuitive and pragmatic in the way they approach their work and tend to be suspicious of and hostile towards over-elaborate theory. The case study that follows, therefore, is intended to make the methodology that has been proposed seem more accessible and practical by showing how it was actually implemented in a classroom. It is not essential for the teacher to include every aspect of the rationale that has been described and exemplified whenever a unit of work which includes a main writing task is planned and implemented. The teacher, featured in the case study, selected particular aspects of the rationale in an action-research study and shaped them to accommodate her own teaching style.

The setting of the unit of work that is to be described was an all-ability high school. The class in question (comprising boys and girls) had reached the Spring term of their fourth year and had been placed in the lowest band according to perceived ability and attainment in English. Pupils in the class would not normally be entered for external examinations; they were a 'non-examination' group whose work was assessed by the school alone. Their morale and self-esteem as regards classroom work and achievement in school were not therefore high.

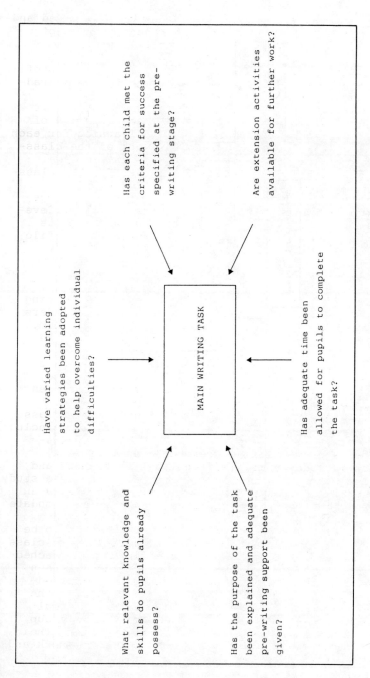

Figure 7.1 Constituent elements of classroom rationale

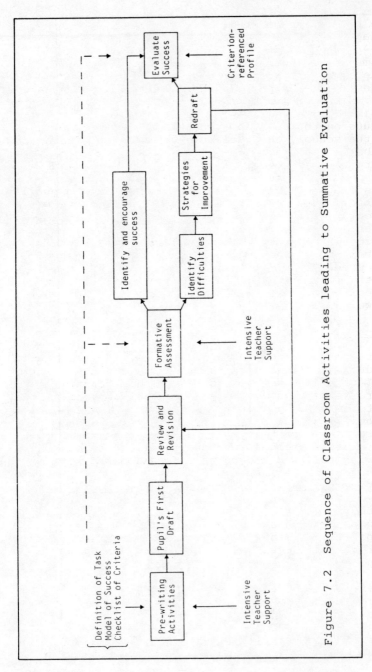

Figure 7.2   Sequence of Classroom Activities leading to Summative Evaluation

The complete unit of work involved the class in the production of a handbook for children in their final year at the local 'feeder' primary school. The purpose of the handbook would be to help the primary school children to understand what life is like in a high school and to help them to make the transition from primary to secondary school.

The unit was made up of a variety of assignments; pupils worked as individuals, in pairs, or in small groups on topics such as the geography and lay-out of the school, the facilities it offered, including clubs and sports, and its rules and regulations. There was, however, one main writing assignment which all pupils had to complete - an account of their first day at secondary school written from a pupil's point of view. An increased sense of purpose was given to this main task by directing it towards a particular audience, namely a group of primary pupils whose school shared the same campus as the high school. These younger children became a focus for pre-writing discussion and at the conclusion of the main assignment a selected group of high school pupils visited them to read their work and answer questions.

Pre-Writing

The initial stimulus for the main task was a short extract from a recording of a television programme produced especially for a schools' audience (*The English Programme:* Thames TV). The extract gave a dramatised account of a young, non-professional writer's retrospective impressions of his new secondary school (Mills 1978). Pupils watched the extract and the teacher then led discussion about the class's initial response to it. A second showing followed and on this occasion the pupils were directed to focus their attention on one particular aspect of the narrator's description - the contrasts between his old primary and his new secondary school. This stimulus succeeded in triggering off pupils' own memories of the event despite some initial grumbles about not being able to recollect anything about something that had happened so long ago.

The teacher then helped the class to form a clearer idea of their intended audience. The children in the adjacent primary school had already been visited as part of the teacher's preparation for the unit. She had primed them (with the help of their own teacher) to ask a variety of questions about the secondary school they would soon be

transferring to, and to voice their doubts and
anxieties about what lay in store for them. These
questions were audio-recorded and then played to
the secondary pupils in their own classroom. A
selection of the questions was also included on a
written worksheet so that they could be referred to
in the course of later work on a range of tasks
(reproduced as Figure 7.3). This strategy proved to
be particularly successful. The writers responded
to the genuineness of the questions; they talked
about their perceptions of their audience and discussed their own replies to the questions the
children had asked. The questions also helped to
create further extension tasks to support the main
assignment. Pupils were directed to choose one area
from the children's questions that they could
respond to and, working individually or in pairs, to
plan a reply which could be included in the final
booklet. These additional tasks were developed
throughout the unit; pupils turned to the work
independently to create variety or as a time-filling
exercise, if they had to wait for the teacher's
attention.

Criteria for success on the main task were made
explicit at this pre-writing stage by means of a
written checklist which was glossed orally in the
classroom for the pupils' benefit. The checklist was
organised under the headings already described in
Chapter Five: *Subject, Point of View, Register,
Organisation,* and *Mechanics.* The guidelines presented under each heading were formulated by the teacher
to suit the requirements of this particular task,
her purposes in setting it, and the nature of the
pupils who were to complete it. Because of the
nature of the class it was organised at one level of
difficulty only. The category labelled *Mechanics*
was deliberately placed at the end of the checklist
so that the surface features of writing would not
assume priority over other elements of the task in
the writers' minds. This final area (perhaps not
surprisingly) was the one about which pupils
expressed the most initial anxiety and in which they
were most lacking in self-confidence. The checklist
is reproduced as Figure 7.4.

A written model chosen to exemplify success
in completing the main task was linked directly to
the initial visual stimulus. It was a transcription
of the author's narrative which had accompanied the
television programme; this narrative had itself been
taken and adapted from the first chapter of the
source autobiography. The text (reproduced as

THE MOVE FROM PRIMARY TO SECONDARY SCHOOL

Pupils in a local Primary class talked recently about what interested and worried them about the coming move to a secondary school. Here are some of the questions they asked. What would you say to help them?

<u>About the school in general</u>
How long did it take you to get to know the school?
Do you like going from class to class instead of staying in one class all day as in Primary school?
Are all the teachers as strict as they're meant to be: like they are on TV?

<u>About the work you do</u>
Is the work really hard?
How much homework do you get?

<u>About the senior pupils</u>
Do you get bossed about by the senior pupils?
Are there any bullies to steer clear of?

<u>About the school uniform</u>
Do you mind having to wear school uniform?

<u>About the activities in the school</u>
What's your opinion on the activities? Should there be more things you could do?
What is your favourite activity?

<u>About school meals and other food</u>
What are the school dinners like?
How are the meals served?
Is there a good variety in the tuck shop?

<u>About the first day at secondary school</u>
What do you remember about your first day?
Do you get ducked on your first day or on birthdays?

Figure 7.3 Worksheet: the move from primary to secondary school.

```
CHECKLIST
```

Use this checklist to help you to produce the best writing that you can.

AUTOBIOGRAPHY: FIRST DAY AT SECONDARY SCHOOL

SUBJECT   1. Describe how you felt and what
                  happened to you on your first
                  day at ....High School.
                  Begin by describing how you
                  arrived at the school on that
                  first day, then describe one
                  or more things which happened.
                  (You could mention how the
                  school looked to you; the people
                  you met and what you had to do).
                  You could finish your account by
                  describing your journey home.

POINT OF   2. Write your composition from your
VIEW   own point of view, keeping in
                  mind that you are writing for
                  10-11 year olds to help them
                  when they come to school for
                  the first time.

REGISTER   3. Try to write about school so
                  that primary pupils will under-
                  stand what you mean. Choose
                  your words carefully and use
                  appropriate grammar.

ORGANISA-   4. You should always try to organ-
TION   ise your sentences into para-
                  graphs. Your writing should be
                  at least 80 words long.

MECHANICS   5. Your spelling should be as
                  careful as possible. Take care
                  too, that your punctuation is
                  clear, especially at the begin-
                  ning and end of sentences. Your
                  handwriting must be clear enough
                  so that your reader will be able
                  to understand it without having
                  to ask what you mean.
```

Figure 7.4    Autobiographical Assignment: Checklist
              of Criteria for Success
```

Appendix B) was therefore first heard as a sound-track and then (later) read aloud by the teacher. Relevant aspects of it were discussed with the whole class and features of the text were later still related to the checklist. The initiative for organising and developing this discussion was taken by the teacher and she summarised aspects of it on the blackboard in the form of a 'geometrical' diagram. This diagram highlighted key events that had made up the writer's experience at his new school and how he had been affected by them so that actual events and the feelings they aroused were juxtaposed.

The summary of key points which the teacher built up on the blackboard as the discussion progressed formed the basis of planning 'maps' which the pupils created for their own first drafts. However, before these maps were drawn up, the class first worked in groups to discuss their own memories of important events that took place during their first days at high school and to recall how they themselves had felt on that occasion. The class then began to work on creating individual planning maps in preparation for the main writing task. The version that the teacher had compiled on the blackboard acted as a model, but pupils completed the different areas of the map in accordance with their own recollections of the important events and the feelings they had experienced in the course of the day in question. One pupil's completed plan is reproduced as Figure 7.5.

Drafting and Re-drafting

When work began on the main writing assignment, the pupils normally worked on their own, although they also frequently collaborated in pairs to compare and review their scripts. Sometimes they were brought together in larger groups, with the teacher present, to discuss the progress they were making. The teacher normally moved round the class, informally monitoring progress and behaviour, and responding to individual requests for help. Classroom routines worked smoothly; on some occasions the pupils entered the classroom, collected their scripts and began work without any overt direction from the teacher. In fact the teacher seldom addressed the class as a whole during this phase of work, except for details of administration such as checking attendance, settling pupils down to work when necessary, or bringing the lesson to a conclusion.

When pupils had completed their first drafts, they submitted them to the teacher for formative

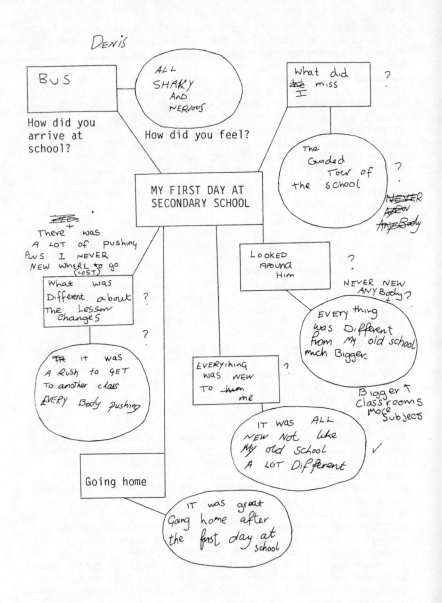

Figure 7.5 Pupil's Planning Map

assessment. For this purpose the teacher made use of both approaches described in Chapter Four. In adopting the 'postal' approach she used the standardised pro-forma already illustrated and discussed (see Figure 4.2) and tried to give as much detailed help and written advice as was feasible. This did not take significantly more time than a normal marking work-load for the class. Individual or small group conferences were carried out in classroom time at the pupils' desks. In highlighting successes, identifying weaknesses and making suggestions for improvements the teacher made frequent references to different aspects of pre-writing preparation, especially the checklist, the model and pupils' own planning maps.

As the class was comparatively small, the teacher was able to give adequate time and attention to all pupils. However, she also deliberately focused attention on a group of four pupils. In this way she was able to give the selected pupils in-depth help in this particular unit of work and gain detailed knowledge of their achievements and difficulties. In a new unit of work a different group of pupils would be selected for this focused attention so that in the course of a term or a session the whole class could be included.

All pupils completed two drafts of their accounts; most completed three. Before and during redrafting the teacher endeavoured to give different kinds of assistance to pupils according to the individual problems they were experiencing and pupils also helped each other. Most of the class had completed this main task at the end of seven lessons devoted to working on it (each lesson being of eighty minutes' duration) and were ready to present their work to the primary school audience. In the teacher's judgement all pupils completed the main task satisfactorily and their success was recorded on individual summative profiles (reproduced as Figure 7.6) which accompanied their folios of collected work.

The classroom work that has been described in outline represents one example only of a single teacher's interpretation of the rationale that has been advocated. In itself it cannot constitute a justification of that rationale. However, the teacher's own evaluation of the unit indicated that the successes that were achieved in this instance were due in part to the intrinsic interest of the subject-matter and the pupils' own understanding and awareness of the topic, in part to the sense of

	SUMMATIVE ASSESSMENT PROFILE		
	YES	NO	COMMENT
Subject			
Described events of first day			
Mentioned at least three elements			
Included reflection on feelings			
Point of View			
Persona correct			
Purpose correct			
Register			
Vocabulary suitable			
Grammar appropriate			
Meaning accessible			
Organisation			
Structured			
Paragraphed appropriately			
Minimum of 80 words			
Mechanics			
Spelling 95% accurate			
Punctuation (especially sentence boundaries) appropriate			
Handwriting legible			

Figure 7.6 Summative Assessment Profile

purpose created by the pupils having to write for a
clearly defined target audience, and in part to the
satisfaction pupils gained both from producing their
successful written accounts and from what they
learned in the course of completing them. To this
list must be added the teacher's own thoroughness
and care in preparing the unit of work and her own
professional skills in implementing it in the classroom. The activities provided by the unit as a
whole were varied and caught the pupils' imagination
and interest; and the standard of ultimate achievement was judged to be high for this particular class.

Two examples of the work finally produced are
the following accounts written by Caroline and John.
Both scripts have been edited in minor ways, but no
major revisions have been made for the purpose of
publication. A detailed case study describing a
third pupil's progress in completing the assignment
(Joseph), can be found in Peacock and Roger (1984
pp.165-185).

MY FIRST DAY AT SECONDARY SCHOOL
It was my first day at a new school and I felt
very lonely, not making new friends. In fact
I had no friends to share my many worries with.
My old friends were all too busy with their
creative dance lessons and their new friends
to worry about me. I was now on my own.

The new school was enormous with strange
surroundings. I felt very lost. I felt very
scared and left out of things. I could not see
my old friends as much as when I was back in
primary school, then we were together as much
as I would want. All my friends deserted me.
I, now left all alone, was desperate for new
friends. I even got bullied and bossed about
by some of the older years including some in
my class and most of the seniors.

On our very first day we did a tour around
the school, with the help of our new guidance
teacher. We got a tour around most of the
subject classes, and I felt really nervous.
We were even told who our new teachers were
going to be.

My new regarstration teacher was Mr M-----
who was also to be our maths teacher for some
time later in the year.

We got told the break-times of the day,
e.g. morning-break and the lunch-break. Our
morning-break started at 10.40 a.m. and
finished at 10.55 a.m. We even got shown our

new toilets, which were situated just outside
the music-block, which was the next one
(building) on the Assembly-block.

Before we went to our Registration-classes
we got separated into different sections into
different houses. My house was C--- and we
were told to go to our separate Reg-rooms,
where there was one for each house. Mr M----
was my Regarstration teacher's name. For the
rest of the morning we were to stay there.

In class, we got our new home-work
diaries and our teacher told us all our facts
and things of importance all about our new
teachers and new subjects.

All of the morning we stayed in our
Registration classes but at lunchtime, which
started at 12.55 and which finished at 1.55
p.m., we were told where the dining-hall was,
and of where to go including about the snacks-
place. There I met and sat beside some people
from my class. As soon as lunch was over we
were all told to go to our normal classes for
the rest of the afternoon.

For my first subject of the afternoon I
got lost about the school. I asked principal-
teachers for help but they were all too busy
for to be ask by me. I also asked older years
- seniors of 4th, 5th and 6th year where I am
to go. They normally gave me a false answer
and then they wrongly directed me to my classes.

I felt rather embarrassed, lonely, sad,
and lost, until I met up with a prefect, who
saved the day. She led me to the right class
at last. On entering my subject class-room I
get rather embarrassed as the situation has
worsened of having to tell the teacher 'that
I was lost'. Then I sat down on my chair, to
sit at ease. It was one of my Maths Subjects.
The afternoon went like a flash and now it was
home-time.

For most of my first-year and the first-
day, I just walked home after school had
finnished and I did not know that there were
any buses that could take me home, so I just
walked home with Helen my big sisger, who was
a prefect at this school, on towards the town
and back to my house.

(Caroline)

As I woke up in the morning I sighed because
it was to be my first day at secondary school.
I looked out of the window and saw children
up very early in their new school uniforms
and feeling very proud of themselves. I
quickly washed and put on my new school
uniform, and went downstairs for my breakfast.
     As I was walking to the bus stop I
thought to myself, what would the bullies be
like or is it just a rumour to make the new-
comers scared of what is in store for them?
The bigger pupils of the school tell you that
they will duck you in the toilet. When I got
the bus stop the L---- twins had their new
school uniforms on as well because it was
their first day at secondary school as well.
     When the bus came there were other children
in new school uniforms starting primary and
secondary school. When we got to the school
it looked huge compared with my primary school.
As we entered the school the air was buzzing
with excited children, who just couldn't wait
for school to start. When we got into the
Assembly Hall there was a sea of green blazers
and jumpers. We were in the Assembly Hall for
the first three periods in the morning. A
teacher started to talk to us about the school
and what goes on in the different buildings.
She talked to us about the school rules and
who were the heads of the different departments.
     After assembly we were told who was our
registration teacher and we were shown where
our classes were. When we got to the class
Mr M---- our registration told us things about
the school and we had to write our timetable
out and this would be our subjects for the
rest of the year.
     We stayed at registration for two periods
then we went to get our dinner. Since it was
our first day we were allowed to go to
dinners before the rest of the school. Myself
and Neale H---- were first in for snacks, he
was a tall boy with curly hair. For the rest
of our dinner hour we went about the school
trying to find different rooms, and getting
to know the school better.
     After dinner we had to go back to normal
timetable and this meant that I had to go to
Maths with Mr K---- who is no longer at the
school. Before I came to the school I thought

that the teachers would be like tyrants and very
strict but I found them very friendly and helpful.

Lesson changing was great because it gave
you the chance to get a breath of fresh air and
a chance to talk to your friends.

School finished half an hour more than the
primary used to finish at. The day dragged on
and it was quite boring because all the teachers
did was take our names and give us new text
books and introduce themselves. When the bell
went at four o'clock I was very relieved to be
going home because the first day is always the
worst.

The next thing I noticed about the school
was when I went to get the bus home. At primary
we lined up in a sensible queue but the high
school pupils went on their buses as a rabble
and it's a wonder nobody got hurt.

I go no homework that night but I knew
when I got it it would be very hard and it
would be a lot more than I was used to at
primary school.

(John)

CHAPTER EIGHT

CONCLUSION: IMPLICATIONS FOR PROFESSIONAL PRACTICE

The approach to the teaching of writing that has
been described and exemplified is thorough and
comprehensive. It is underpinned by coherent theory
in its conceptualisation of the nature of the writing
process and classroom pedagogy. However, although
efforts have been made to ensure some measure of
flexibility so that the overall rationale can be
interpreted in different ways and the approach
adapted by a variety of teachers working in different contexts, it would be unrealistic to assume that
the procedures which have been advocated can simply
be grafted on to a teacher's existing beliefs and
professional practice without difficulty. Some of
the changes needed in order to accept and implement
the recommended rationale could be fundamental. The
purpose of this final chapter therefore is to
consider the nature of some of the most important
changes that may be required in professional thinking
and practice if an individual teacher, or a department or school, were to seek to implement the
systematic approach to the teaching of writing that
has been described.
        One source of fundamental difficulties is
likely to be a conflict of beliefs and values concerning the nature of the teacher's classroom role.
If the proposed rationale is to be successfully
implemented, it is evident that a teacher needs
initially to accept the desirability of a structured
and systematic approach to teaching and learning, to
believe in its value, and have faith in its effectiveness. If such an acceptance based on prior knowledge
and experience is not forthcoming (and as discussion
in earlier chapters indicated, this cannot be assumed)
a genuine openness to trial and critical evaluation
would be an essential pre-condition for success.
        Central to the proposed rationale is the

teacher's instructional role in the classroom. The
approach may therefore be perceived as over-directive,
too much dominated by the teacher at the expense of
the learner. The pupil's complementary role as a
learner is not undervalued - successful teaching is
obviously dependent upon successful learning - but
an acceptance of the importance of explicit teaching
or instruction may require for some practising
teachers a shift of perspective in their planning
and pedagogy. This shift of perspective may be
perceived as bringing about a more directive, and
therefore less child-centred, approach to education.
In adopting the rationale teachers would not as a
result have to value any less what the individual
child brings to the classroom in the way of knowledge,
interests or life experience, nor would they be
required to return to traditional directive or
didactic teaching methods. But in some cases they
might need to value more highly what it is they
wish to teach, and to explore more fully how the
required knowledge, skill and understanding may
most effectively be communicated to their pupils.
   As a consequence of this fundamental shift of
perspective concerning their classroom role,
teachers may need to adopt a less open approach to
what is (explicitly) taught and learned, set less
ambitious and more clearly defined targets for
classroom work and cover a more limited curricular
field in the course of a school session. If these
changes can be negotiated, the rewards that ensue
could be significant. Teachers would be able as a
result to formulate and communicate to their pupils
(and others) attainable objectives for their classroom work and evaluate more effectively their own
and their pupils' success. As one interviewed
teacher, who piloted the proposed rationale in his
own classroom, commented at the conclusion of the
trial:

> *... for a long time I've felt that as English*
> *teachers we were far too vague ... you know,*
> *we gave pupils kind of vague instructions and*
> *if they could work out what we really wanted*
> *behind that, as it were, they got bonus marks*
> *... I'd the notion of being able to say to*
> *pupils, 'Right now what you must do are the*
> *following things ... you could also consider*
> *doing these and then there are these beyond it,*
> *as it were ... but if you do the first lot,*
> *you pass ... you've done it ... you've been*
> *successful ...' and then beginning to assess*
> *them on what they've done ... I think that's a*

> *huge step ... so that they know what they're*
> *doing and they see how it all fits in...*
> *It's a lot of work and in some ways it narrows*
> *the course ... There will still be room for*
> *stuff which is done just for fun or kind of*
> *extensions of that ... it doesn't all have to*
> *be done that way ... but to have a course which*
> *will be a departmental course agreed upon, where*
> *you can assure yourself, your Board of Manage-*
> *ment, parents, pupils, that if you follow a*
> *four-year course with this school, then at*
> *this level you will have done the following and*
> *you will be able to do the following ... at*
> *this level ... I think that's a ... I think*
> *that's a marvellous thing.*
>
> (Peacock and Roger 1984 p.207)

An additional related problem may be the teacher's
degree of willingness to accept that all pupils (no
matter what their background or perceived abilities)
should achieve success. We are all of us so cond-
itioned by past experience to accept a norm-
referenced conceptualisation of success that we feel
that if everyone in the class is to succeed, then
somehow the notion of success is itself devalued;
we believe that success must be accompanied by a
measure of failure. To accept that all pupils
should succeed in school does not necessarily involve
a utopian belief that all pupils are ultimately
capable of achieving the same levels and kinds of
success. But teachers do have to be prepared to
plan their classroom work in such a way that it is
possible for every child to experience some form of
success and to help them to become aware that they
are making visible progress in their writing development. An acceptance of the importance of organising
classroom work to clarify and emphasise individual
achievement, and the use of criterion referenced
assessment procedures to analyse and communicate
different kinds of success to the learner in order
to promote further development are likely (as has
been argued) to improve children's self-esteem and
motivation. But more importantly for the present
discussion, the acceptance of this approach is
likely to influence the teacher's whole attitude
to how work is planned and implemented in the classroom. The teacher's task is perceived in a distinctive way and past experience of different kinds
of curriculum development in schools suggests that
fundamental changes in professional beliefs and
attitudes are not normally easily negotiated or

accepted by teachers. (Stenhouse 1975 Chapter 14)
    Even when teachers do accept the need for these
essential changes of attitude and belief, the
practical problems that are likely to confront them
in implementing the rationale are still considerable.
The procedures that have been advocated are obviously
demanding in the thoroughness of planning and
preparation that is required. They are demanding
too in terms of the repertoire of varied learning
strategies that a teacher has to be able to exploit
in order to help individual children to learn effectively. But the procedures can be demanding also in
the professional skills that are required to achieve
the necessary flexibility of organisation and
management in the classroom that enables children to
work in different ways and at different speeds.
Unless such flexibility is already a feature of the
teacher's habitual practice and the pupils' accepted
routines the change to this mode of organisation can
be difficult and stressful. One experienced teacher
who piloted the rationale in a secondary school, for
example, made the following comments in interview:

> *... then I gave them another exercise and in
> this case I gave them a clear checklist ...
> well I thought it was clear anyway... which had
> related to the different levels of criteria
> ... and they came in today and they milled
> about and they said 'What are we going to do?'
> and 'Will I redraft this?' and so on ... and
> it was all total disaster ... a mess ... Now
> clearly there's something ... I've missed
> something there ... I haven't trained them
> properly ... so em, what I learned from work
> with you is fine in the abstract, you know, in
> terms of planning and approach ... and I'm sure
> it's useful ... good stuff ... but the actual
> management of it ... I'm still left with big
> problems ... which are partly mine and partly
> to do with some of the pupils.*
>   (Peacock and Roger 1984 p.204)

Perhaps the most pressing practical problem, though,
which is likely to face the teacher who seeks to
adopt and implement the rationale is simply lack of
time. Adequate time is needed to plan and prepare
work; it is needed also to assess work thoroughly
and discuss achievement and progress with individual
pupils; and adequate classroom time is essential
for all pupils to complete a main writing task
satisfactorily. It is unlikely that additional

professional time will be created for teachers trying to bring about changes in their classroom practice; any solution will lie in the more effective use of the time that is already available. Certainly, pilot work in classrooms suggested that both teachers and pupils found the high measure of concentration on a written text and the detailed attention given to the process of drafting and redrafting to be demanding and tiring.

To help teachers overcome these practical problems when they begin to plan and implement units of classroom work as advocated in the rationale, ideally, additional professional time and resources need to be made available. However, if this is not forthcoming, at the very least additional psychological support needs to be provided within the department or school (or from an outside agency). Teams of teachers need to share the demands of planning, to discuss the nature of key writing tasks and the criteria they will apply to pupils' scripts when they evaluate success; they need to share their difficulties and help each other to find solutions when they come to implement schemes of work in the classroom.

If these practical problems can be overcome, the professional gains to be won could be considerable. Teachers of writing would remain in control of and responsible for what is to be taught and learned in their own classrooms. But they would also be more coherent and convincing when they sought to make explicit to those within and beyond the school their aims in the teaching of writing and the nature of their pupils' achievements, brought about as a direct result of their classroom work. Professional esteem would thereby be enhanced. Many children too could experience increased satisfaction from their classroom work because of their awareness of what they had achieved in learning to write and their sense of continuing progress.

Conflicts in educational values and the practical problems of classroom implementation will not be resolved simply or quickly. A major purpose of this book has been to stimulate discussion and debate about these problems. And clearly they are applicable to much more than simply the teaching of writing in schools. It is hoped too that the preceding chapters will have provided encouragement and support to those teachers who are already committed to a more systematic, structured approach in their classroom work or who are in some measure dissatisfied with their present professional practice

in the teaching of writing. A third principal aim
in developing the arguments and presenting illustration in earlier chapters has been to encourage
all teachers of writing to reflect on the rationale
and methodology they currently accept for their
classroom work and to question its validity and
effectiveness. If these three major purposes are
achieved, then the efforts involved will be worthwhile.

APPENDIX A

RESCUE GROUPS EASE THE CRISIS
By Alison Jenkins

The Stirling weather at last seems to be getting
milder and the snow which has fallen over the past
few weeks is slowly melting away.

But as temperatures rose many families again
found themselves with burst pipes - some of them
for the second or third time in a matter of weeks.

Some of the council tenants who have had two
or three burst pipes have now become quite experienced at basic plumbing.

Mr Carl Donachie, depute director of the district council's housing department, said on Monday
that many tenants are now beginning to understand a
little about elementary plumbing.

"Many tenants can now switch off the main water
supply themselves and they seem to be coping better
until the plumbers arrive," he commented.

"Again we have had an absolutely excellent response from friends and neighbours of families who
have been affected by bursts.

"But with two families we had no alternative
but to rehouse them."

Mr Donachie estimated that the housing department has had to deal with more than 4,000 emergency
calls over the past few weeks.

"I have not seen anything like it while I have
been in this job and many of my colleagues have not
either", he added.

"All we can do is hope that the thaw continues.
We have been in touch with the Met office in
Glasgow and they have indications that it will con-
tinue for a couple of days at least."

Central Regional Council departments have played
a major role over the past two weeks in helping re-
lieve many of the problems.

Plumbers from the direct works department were
placed on standby to go to the aid of district
council workmen battling against a flood of burst
pipes and the school meals service was ready to step
in with emergency supplies of food for families made
homeless during the crisis.

The bulk of the regional council's contribution
has however been made by the social work department
which has given support in various forms to the three
district authorities - Clackmannan, Falkirk and
Stirling.

The department has been particularly busy

checking people at risk and helping the district councils establish emergency centres where day and temporary accommodation would be available for homeless families and single people.

By the weekend places had been found in Central Regional Council old folks homes for 31 elderly and handicapped people. Unable to survive in their own homes, their safety depended on them being taken into care by the regional authority.

The milder weather over the weekend meant less work for the Automobile Association.

It received as many as 50 calls a day less than in the previous two weeks in the Stirling area. But a spokesman for the AA in Edinburgh said that the main problems were still with flat batteries and cars freezing up because no anti-freeze had been put in.

From the *Stirling Observer* 30th December 1981
(Reprinted with permission)

APPENDIX B

FIRST DAY

A tearless farewell from Primary School and a long
hot six weeks holiday culminating in a sleepless
night had resulted in my sitting outside the
administrative offices of Effingham Road Comprehensive School. Actually, due to a previously booked
holiday, I missed the first week at Effingham Road
and forever after wondered if I'd missed some vital
explanation during that week, some single phrase or
few words which would have made everything add up,
made everything clear and given some meaning and
reason to the next five years I would spend there.

All I had actually missed was a guided tour
on my first day. The first year boys, without the
hindrance of the other years, who started the next
day, were shown the wonders of the premises ...
But I had missed out on that tour and it was three
years before I knew my way about the school. Now
I was alone with my brand new briefcase, empty save
for a fountain pen. There was no group of boys to
hide behind and no friends to share my worries
with...

The thing that struck me most on that first day
was the newness of everything. Everything steel
and glass, everything white and clean. It had none
of the cosiness of my primary classroom with its
rabbits at the back and painted pictures on the wall.
Lesson changes here were hustle and bustle, aggress-
ive shoulders pushing in the corridors and bodies
jostling on the stairs ...

It was a very long day, the way it always is
when you are in totally new surroundings and your
mind does not get a chance to slip into a routine.
I arrived home, legs aching - it was over a mile's
walk. My arms ached too, my bag full of fat hard-
back books with torn pages. A new worry was stir-
ring in my mind, all that homework. Homework kept
you from playing in the streets or watching television.

But I did watch television that evening of
the first day. On a variety show a comedian told
a joke about a little boy after his first day at
primary school. His mother said, 'Now we're not
going to have all that crying and screaming when you
go tomorrow, are we?' And he said, 'You don't mean
I have to go again, do you?'

From *A Comprehensive Education,* by Roger Mills (1978)
(Centreprise Trust Limited pp.9-15) (Reprinted with
permission)

REFERENCES

Applebee, A.N. (1981) *Writing in the Secondary School: English and the Content Areas* NCTE Research Report No.21, National Council of Teachers of English, Urbana.

Bartz, F.K. (1976) 'Getting Students to Use Detail' in Long, L. (ed.) (1976) q.v.

Bloom, B.S. (1976) *Human Characteristics and School Learning* McGraw-Hill, New York.

Britton, J., Burgess, T., Martin N., McLeod A. and Rosen, H. (1975) *The Development of Writing Abilities (11-18)* Schools Council Research Studies, Macmillan Education, Houndmills.

Carter, C. (ed.) (1982) *Structuring for Success in the English Classroom: classroom practices in teaching English 1981-82* National Council of Teachers of English, Urbana.

Christenbury, L. (1982) 'Structuring the Classroom for Peer Revision of Composition' in Carter, C. (ed.) q.v.

Clapp, O.H. (ed.) (1975) *On Righting Writing: classroom practices in teaching English 1975-76* 13th Report of Committee on Classroom Practices, National Council of Teachers of English, Urbana.

Cooper, C.R. and Odell, L. (1977) *Evaluating Writing: Describing, Measuring, Judging* National Council of Teachers of English, Urbana.

Cotterell, G. 'A Remedial Approach to a Spelling Disability' in Wade, B. and Wedell, K. (eds.) (1974) q.v.

Doughty, P., Pearce, J. and Thornton, G. (1972) *Exploring Language* Schools Council/Edward Arnold, London

Frederiksen, C.H. and Dominic, J.F. (eds.) (1981) *Writing: the nature, development and teaching of written communication: Volume Two - Writing: Process, Development and Communication* Erlbaum, New Jersey

138

Galanter, E. (1966) *Textbook of Elementary Psychology*
    Holden Day, San Francisco.

Haley-James S. (ed.) (1981) *Perspectives on Writing
    in Grades 1 - 8* National Council of Teachers of
    English, Urbana.

Hillocks, G., (1984) 'What Works in Teaching Composi-
    tion: a meta-analysis of experimental treat-
    ment studies' *American Journal of Education*
    November pp.133-170.

Howell, K.W. and Kaplan, J.S. (1980) *Diagnosing Basic
    Skills: a handbook for deciding what to teach*
    Charles E. Merrill, Columbus.

Humes, A. (1983) 'Research on the Composing Process'
    Review of Educational Research 53 Number 2
    pp.201-216.

Jarman, C. (1979) *The Development of Handwriting
    Skills: a book of resources for teachers*
    Blackwell, Oxford.

Long, L. (ed.) (1976) *Writing Exercises from
    'Exercise Exchange'* National Council of Teachers
    of English, Urbana.

McAlpine, A.N. (1982) 'An Investigation of Teachers'
    Written and Oral Comments on Pupils' Learning
    Performances in English Teaching', Unpublished
    Ph.D. Thesis, University of Stirling.

McLeod, A.(1982) 'Writing, Dialect and Linguistic
    Awareness' in Eyers S., and Richmond, J. (eds.)
    Becoming Our Own Experts: the Vauxhall Papers
    Inner London Education Authority: English
    Centre.

Mills, R. (1978) *A Comprehensive Education 1965-
    1975* Centreprise Trust Limited, London

Moorhouse, C. (1977) *Helping Adults to Spell*
    Adult Literacy Resource Agency, London

Nold, E.W. (1981) 'Revising' in Frederiksen, C.H.
    and Dominic, J.F. (eds.) (1981) q.v. (Chapter
    5).

Onion, M.K. (1976) 'Preparing to Write Clear Direc-
    tions' in Long, L. (ed.) (1976) q.v.

Peacock, C. and Roger, A. (1984) *Success in Writing: a classroom study with slower learning pupils in three Scottish secondary schools (S3/S4)* Scottish Curriculum Development Service: Moray House College of Education, Edinburgh.

Peters, M.L. (1967) *Spelling: Caught or Taught?* Routledge and Kegan Paul, London

Roberts, B. (1979) *The Language of Growth: the New Brunswick Writing Assessment Program* New Brunswick Department of Education (Evaluation Branch)

Roberts, G.R. and Lunzer, E.A. (1968) 'Reading and Learning to Read' in Lunzer E.A. and Morris J.F. (eds.) (1968) *Development in Human Learning* Staples Press, London.

Roger, A. (1982a) 'The Teaching of Writing: teachers' accounts of their professional practice' Unpublished mimeograph, University of Stirling.

Roger, A. (1982b) Classroom Transcripts: unpublished data 'Language Skills in English' Project, Scottish Education Department/University of Stirling.

Rowntree, D. (1977) *Assessing Students: How Shall We Know Them?* Harper and Row, London.

Sands, M. and Kerry, T. (eds.) (1982) *Mixed Ability Teaching* Croom Helm, London.

Scardamalia, M., Bereiter, C. and Fillion, B. (1981) *Writing for Results: a sourcebook of consequential composing activities* Ontario Institute for Studies in Education (Curriculum Series 44)

Shaughnessy, M.P. (1977) *Errors and Expectations: a guide for the teacher of basic writing* Oxford University Press.

Shuman, R.B. (1975) 'I Swapped Words for Stories' in Clapp, O.H. (ed.) (1975) q.v.

Slater, E. (1981) 'The Text-based Lesson in the English Classroom'. Unpublished Honours Dissertation, University of Stirling.

Smith, D.E.P., Smith, J.M. and Brink, J.R. (1976-1978) *A Technology of Reading and Writing* Four Volumes, Academic Press, New York.

Smith, F. (1982) *Writing and the Writer* Heinemann Educational, London.

Southgate, V., Arnold, H. and Johnson, S. (1981) *Extending Beginning Reading* Schools Council/ Heinemann Educational, London.

Spencer, E. (1983) *Writing Matters Across the Curriculum* Scottish Council for Research in Education/Hodder and Stoughton, Sevenoaks.

Stenhouse, L. (1975) *An Introduction to Curriculum Research and Development* Heinemann Educational, London.

Wade, B. and Wedell, K. (eds.) (1974) *Spelling: Task and Learner, Educational Review* Occasional Publications Number 5, University of Birmingham.

aims in the teaching of
    writing 1, 68, 83, 96,
    111, 130, 133
assessment
    criterion-referenced
    113-114, 131
    formative 43-44, 50,
    78, 110, 112, 123
    marks and grades 112-
    113
    norm-referenced 113,
    131
    profile for 48, 109,
    114, 123
    summative 43, 112,
    123
    teachers' responses
    43, 45-46, 52
    see also evaluation

categories of writing
    16-18, 106
    transactional-poetic
    16
    informational,
    personal, imaginat-
    ive 17
    writing without
    composing 17, 93
checklist of criteria
    for success 66, 69,
    108, 118, 132
children's writing
    'Moment of Fear' 3
    2G Visit Tower of
    London 5-7

'A Fit with the Reds'
    15
'Let's Play Poison'
    39-40
'Getting Up on a Cold
    Morning' 61
'My Views on Violence'
    62
'A Disaster' 79-81
'Rescue Groups Ease
    the Crisis' 99
'First Day at Secondary
    School' 125-128
classroom management 54-
    56, 75, 77, 82, 109,
    110, 121, 132
classroom methodology
    changing practice 129,
    132-133
    cognitive approach 19,
    92
    drafting and redrafting
    35, 78-84, 121-123,
    133
    holistic approach 2-4,
    8, 19, 111
    'lock-step' 110
    'steering groups' 59
    sub-skills approach 2,
    8, 18
    teacher's role 2, 111,
    129-130, 133
classroom 'rules' 29, 53,
    55, 78, 132
classroom writing tasks
    case-study 117-125

classroom writing tasks
(continued)
    dictation 31, 93
    level of difficulty
    59-62, 107, 108, 109
    'mechanical' and
    'informational' 17-18
    pupils' perception of
    93, 95, 97, 111
    range 55, 70, 108,
    110, 118
    task analysis 68
    teachers' planning
    110, 131, 132, 133
    teachers' rules 29,
    53, 55
'climate for learning'
    2, 78, 104, 105, 111
cognitive approach to
    teaching 19, 92
composing 25, 26-30
    cognitive demands 27,
    42, 60
    communicative
    setting 14, 28, 41
    contextual constraints
    29
    explicitness 79-80,
    94-95
    linguistic demands 27,
    42, 60
    visual encoding 42, 71
    writer's subjectivity
    30, 102
conference (teacher-
    pupil) 46-50, 79, 84,
    87, 123
'correctness' in language
    15-16
criteria for success 51,
    53, 66, 68-69, 78,
    108, 112-113, 133
criterion-referenced
    assessment
    113-114, 131
'cybernetic hypothesis'
    20
    application to
    writing 22, 51-52
    feedback loop 20,
    51-52

    'plans' 20, 25, 52, 68,
    97
    test-operate-test 21,
    30, 35

dictation 31, 39

editing 35, 90, 92
    see also redrafting,
    reviewing, revising
evaluation 42, 96, 108,
    111, 112-114, 123,
    133
    self-evaluation 7, 55,
    108, 111
    see also assessment

feedback 20, 24-25, 50,
    52, 105, 112
'flotation' approach (to
    assessment) 52-53, 58,
    68
'foils' 96
formative assessment
    after writing 46-50
    criteria for success
    51, 53, 66, 68-69, 78,
    108, 112-113, 133
    connection with pre-
    writing 53, 68, 123
    during writing 44-46
    'flotation' approach
    52-53, 58, 68
    focusing strategy 56,
    123
    management of 54-56
    peer-revision 90-92
    'postal' method 46-50,
    84, 123
    'profile' 48
    reference to a model 70
    reference to a plan 73
    teacher-pupil con-
    ference 46-50, 79, 84,
    87, 123
    teacher responses 43,
    45-46, 47-48, 50, 52,
    53, 80-81
    teacher's role 84-85,
    89

grapholect 27

handwriting 34, 69
holistic approach to
   teaching 2-4, 8, 19,
   111

key-words 72, 79, 98

learning styles 77-78,
   109

'map game' 94-95
marks and grades 112-113
mental rehearsal 31, 41,
   93-94
model of success 70, 84,
   90, 95-96, 98, 108,
   113, 118
motivation 1, 4, 82, 98,
   100-101, 104, 111-
   112, 131

norm-referenced assess-
   ment 113, 131

peer-revision 90-92, 98,
   101, 103
planning (before
   writing)
   discussion 72, 73, 79
   key-words 72, 79, 98
   'maps' 73, 79
   outline notes 72
   teacher explanation
   71-72, 79
'plans' (cognitive) 20,
   25, 52, 68, 97
   see also
   'cybernetic hypo-
   thesis'
'postal approach'(to
   assessment) 46-50,
   84, 123
practice in writing
   2-4, 92-95, 100
pre-writing activities
   100-101, 111
   achieving clarity
   94, 97
   checklist 66, 69,

108, 118, 132
   discussion 73-76, 79,
   97, 117, 121
   explanation 63-66, 79,
   118
   planning 71-74, 79, 89-
   90, 121
   questioning 66
   selecting criteria for
   success 66, 71, 108,
   111, 118
   sense of audience 117
   stimuli for writing 2,
   58, 71, 117, 118
   using a model of
   success 70, 84, 90,
   95-96, 98, 108, 113,
   118
   worksheets 118
profile (for assessment)
   48, 109, 114, 123
punctuation 32-33, 69,
   79-80, 102-103, 109
pupils' progress 80-81,
   82, 104, 105, 109, 124,
   133

rationale (theoretical) 9,
   105, 114, 130
redrafting 35, 46-47, 78-
   84, 98, 121-123, 132
   see also editing,
   reviewing, revising
register (in language) 4,
   15-16, 42, 70
reviewing 25, 34-36
   see also editing, re-
   drafting, revising
revising 34, 83, 85, 90,
   94, 95
   see also editing, re-
   drafting, reviewing

'self-dictation' 31, 41,
   93, 94
'self-shaping' 96, 108
sense of audience 4, 16,
   28-29, 33, 41, 79, 102,
   117, 124
spelling 32, 69, 79-80,
   93, 94, 99, 100,

spelling (continued)
101, 109
auditory discrimina-
tion 94
visual recall 94
stimuli for writing 2, 58,
71, 117, 118
success in writing 130
concept of success 106,
109, 130
discriminating between
success and failure
95-97
motivation of
success 82, 112
success on task 107,
112, 125
'targets' for success
96
summative assessment 43,
112, 123
see also evaluation

task analysis 68
teaching strategies 77,
109, 132
achieving clarity 94-95
competitive proof-
reading 102
demonstration 84-90
dictation 93
discriminating 95-97
'foils' 96
inductive approaches
97, 103
peer-revision 90-92,
98, 101, 103
practice 92-95, 100
problem-solving 100,
104, 111
spelling corrections
93, 100
to improve
punctuation 102-103
teaching styles 104, 109,
114, 130
teaching writing
see classroom method-
ology
test-operate-test 21, 30,
35

see also 'cybernetic
hypothesis'
time for assessment 123,
132
for preparation 132
on task 82, 109-110,
112, 123
transcribing 25, 30-34,
93
handwriting/keyboard
skills 34
mental rehearsal 31,
41, 93, 94
punctuation 32-33
spelling 32

word processors 84
writing curriculum -
sequential 107
'spiral' 107
see also categories of
writing
writer's 'repertoire' 16,
106, 108
writing process
communication of
meaning 4, 8, 12-18
composing 25, 26-30
relationship with
talking 12-14
reviewing 25, 34-36,
83-85, 90
sense of audience 4,
16, 28-29, 33, 41,
79, 102, 117, 124
transcribing 25, 30-
34
writing tasks
see classroom writing
tasks